The Best of 2016

Foreign Affairs December 2016

Our Top Picks from Print and Web

TABLE OF CONTENTS

BEST OF PRINT

BEST OF WEB

Equality and American Democracy

Why Politics Trumps Economics

Danielle Allen

Evicted: Robert Lindneux's 1942 The Trail of Tears.

Since the trend toward rising economic inequality in the United States became apparent in the 1990s, scholars and commentators have heatedly debated its causes and consequences. What has been less evident is a vigorous positive discussion about what equality means and how it might be pursued.

Up through the middle of the nineteenth century, Americans saw equality and liberty as mutually reinforcing ideals. Political equality, shored up by economic equality, was the means by which democratic citizens could secure their liberty. The Declaration of Independence treats the equal capacity of human beings to make judgments about their situations and those of their communities as the basis for popular government and identifies the people's shared right to alter or abolish existing political institutions as the only true security for their freedom. And Abraham Lincoln famously summed up the founding as the birth of a nation "conceived in Liberty, and dedicated to the proposition that all men are created equal."

As the historian James Hutson has shown, many of the founders understood the achievement of political liberty to require some meaningful degree of economic equality. One of the most important policy achievements of the era was the elimination in most states of primogeniture laws, a favorite cause of Thomas Jefferson. Thomas Paine advocated giving a cash grant to every man and woman on turning 21 and an annual pension to every person aged 50 and older, both to be funded through an estate tax. And even John Adams, who thought that the franchise should be limited to property holders, nonetheless believed that class should be defined as broadly as possible in order to avoid turning the new country into an oligarchy. In May 1776, he wrote to a fellow politician, "The only possible Way then of preserving the Ballance of Power on the side of equal Liberty and public Virtue, is to make the Acquisition of Land easy to every Member of Society: to make a Division of the Land into Small Quantities, So that the Multitude may be possessed of landed Estates."

The founders didn't just espouse economic equality; they lived it. According to the historian Allan Kulikoff, at the time of the Revolution, more than 70 percent of white households in western counties, such as the Piedmont area of Virginia and newly settled regions of Maine, New Jersey, Pennsylvania, and even New York, owned land. In eastern counties, property ownership had started to slip but still neared 60 percent. The new nation's successful development of political equality and liberty rested on a historically unprecedented level of economic equality within the white population.

The country's leaders, moreover, chose to perpetuate this situation through public policy. The egalitarian land distributions arranged in the Northwest Territory through the land ordinances of the 1780s may be the most famous case, but they were not alone. From 1805 to 1833, for example, Georgia distributed most of its land to white men, widows, and orphans through random lotteries.

But this, of course, is where the story turns sour. Where did Georgia's officials get that land to give away? From Native Americans, driven out of their homes thanks to the strenuous efforts of Andrew Jackson and others. Georgia's remarkably equal distribution of property is thus known by historians as "the Cherokee land lottery." Both the levelers among the founders and their critics agreed on where the wealth necessary for the new nation would come from: the expropriation of Native Americans, as well as from slave and indentured labor.

When the French traveler Alexis de Tocqueville visited the United States in the early 1830s, he was struck by the egalitarian nature of the young nation—both in its culture and in the distribution of wealth. And many in those days recognized that in order for political equality to persist over time, it needed to be matched by some degree of economic equality. This is no less true today than it was then. Now, however, Americans must find a way to achieve such equality without relying on extraction and appropriation.

LIBERTY VS. EQUALITY

In contrast to the early years of the republic, during which equality and liberty were understood to reinforce each other, by the middle of the twentieth century, it had become commonplace to invoke the idea of an "eternal conflict" between the two values, as a classic 1960 libertarian article put it. What happened in the interim? The rise of industrialization, which changed the balance of power among land, labor, and capital.

Responding to the transformations they saw around them in the early days of the Industrial Revolution, Marx and Engels predicted in The Communist Manifesto that "the proletariat will use its political supremacy to wrest, by degrees, all capital from the bourgeoisie, to centralize all instruments of production in the hands of the State." They continued: "Of course, in the beginning this cannot be effected except by means of despotic inroads on the rights of property and on the conditions of bourgeois production." Although Marx described his goal with the vocabulary of emancipation, his cause became linked to the ideal of equality—which soon lost its political meaning and came to be generally understood in economic terms. Economic equality thus came to be seen as something achievable only via "despotic inroads" on liberties such as the right to property. Fusing this with social Darwinism, the late-nineteenth-century thinker William Graham Sumner captured the new view succinctly: "Let it be understood that we cannot go outside of this alternative: liberty, inequality, survival of the fittest; not-liberty, equality, survival of the unfittest."

WIKIMEDIA COMMONS

An engineering company in Germany during the Industrial Revolution, 1868.

The idea that liberty and equality are necessarily in conflict with each other became a staple of Cold War rhetoric that cast free-market capitalism (alongside religiosity) as the defining feature of the political system of the United States and totalitarian equalization (alongside atheism) as the defining feature of the Soviet Union.

There are so few clichés about equality because Americans have spent so little time dwelling on the subject.

In American public discourse, clichés abound for expressing what freedom means. "Give me liberty or give me death." "Don't tread on me." "It's a free country." "A man's home is his castle." "Doing what you like is freedom; liking what you do is happiness." But clichés about equality are much rarer, pretty much limited to "All men are created equal" and "One person, one vote." George Orwell argued that clichés indicate the corruption of thought by politics; speakers relying on them reveal an absence of original mental effort. But surely the absence of clichés indicates an even greater absence of thought. There are so few clichés about equality because Americans have spent so little time dwelling on the subject.

SPHERES OF JUSTICE

The first task in any project of recovering an ideal of equality is to recognize that the concept requires further specification. When speakers invoke equality, do they mean moral, political, social, or economic equality? Even in the economic sphere alone, are they concerned with equality of outcomes or of opportunity? And what do they assume about the relationships among these different types of equality, or "spheres of justice," as the political theorist Michael Walzer has dubbed them?

Moral equality is the idea that all human beings have the same fundamental worth and deserve the same basic protection of rights. The framework of international human rights law rests on and captures this idea.

Political equality is the ideal that all citizens have equal rights of access to political institutions. It is most commonly defined as requiring civil and political rights—to freely associate and express oneself, to vote, to hold office, and to serve on juries. These are important rights, and protecting them from infringement is critical. But a richer notion of egalitarian empowerment would also consider whether society is structured so as to empower citizens to enter the fray of a politically competitive system. Questions about a right to education, for instance, would come in here, as would questions about campaign finance and electoral redistricting, which could impede the potential for truly democratic representation.

Social equality involves the quality of social relations and associational life. Are neighborhoods integrated? Do equally qualified individuals have equal chances at jobs and valuable positions in society? During the civil rights movement, African American activists often had to set aside any claim to be pursuing social equality in order to get whites to support a project of securing political equality. The bargain was, to put it crudely, that the vote, the lunch counter, and public schools could be desegregated as long as that did not lead to greater rates of interracial marriage or social relations. Of course, that wasn't true, but at that point, explicit pursuit of social equality was a bridge too far. The Black Lives Matter campaign has now put the question of social equality squarely on the table, where it ought to have been all along.

Demonstrators in the Poor People's March at Lafayette Park and Connecticut Avenue in Washington, D.C., June 1968.

Economic equality, finally, has come to the fore thanks to recent trends, with all the complexities and conundrums of its lack. There is now a broad consensus, for example, that straight equalization of economic resources can be achieved only at the cost of extreme, unjust, and counterproductive restrictions on personal liberty and a significant reduction of aggregate economic growth. This doesn't mean, however, that no egalitarian economic policy is possible, nor does it excuse us from trying to introduce into economic policy discussions notions of justice, fairness, and opportunity. The political philosopher John Rawls, for example, made compelling arguments that it is moral to pursue economic policies that generate inequalities, but only if they benefit the worse off in absolute terms, or at least do them no absolute harm.

Treating each domain of equality on its own terms has its uses. But it is also important to treat them together, asking how they relate to one another and how they should be prioritized.

POLITICS FIRST

The early-nineteenth-century political philosopher Benjamin Constant famously argued that there was a critical difference between the liberty of the ancients and that of the moderns. The ancients, he averred, sought above all the freedom to participate in politics and to control their institutions, whereas the moderns preferred to be free from the burdens of politics in order to pursue their commercial enterprises and material pleasures. (Americans heard a strange echo of this argument when U.S. President George W. Bush, in the wake of the 9/11 attacks, called on them to continue their commercial activity in fulfillment of their civic duty.)

We need a virtuous circle in which political equality supports institutions that, in turn, support social and economic equality.

In modern mass democracies, it is indubitably harder to participate meaningfully in politics than it would have been in ancient Greek city-states or even republican Rome. This fact has led philosophers from John Stuart Mill to Isaiah Berlin to Rawls to accept the view that what we really need are experts who can set up a framework to protect citizens' liberties and material interests while they go about the business of living as they choose.

Yet this is to ask people to abandon the most powerful instrument available to them to effect their safety and happiness, namely politics. For if there is now a consensus that full equalization of economic resources would require extreme and costly restrictions on liberty, there is also now a consensus that there is no such thing as a totally free market. To function well, markets depend on rules, norms, and regulations, backed by law and the power of the state, and it is politics that determines what those rules, norms, and regulations will be. Politics trumps economics, in other words, or at least sets the terms according to which the economic game is played. So discussions of economic equality cannot be contained within the economic sphere alone and need to come back around, in the end, to the political sphere.

Discussions of political equality, in turn, can and should bring economics into play, including the prospect of political contestation around issues of economic fairness. In other words, policies that secure political equality can have an effect on income inequality by increasing a society's political competitiveness and thereby affecting "how technology evolves, how markets function, and how the gains from various different economic arrangements are distributed," as the scholars Daron Acemoglu and James

Robinson have noted. This is precisely the linkage the economist Amartya Sen called attention to with his research on the politics of famine in India, pointing out that there were some mass starvations under colonialism, despite the country's great agricultural fertility, but there have not been any under democracy.

And there are other, even more important reasons for prioritizing political equality, such as the argument from moral equality that the best way to ensure that each person can be the author of his or her own life is by giving everyone an ownership stake in political institutions. Approaching egalitarianism through political equality rather than other routes leads to two further questions: How does one's status within the political realm relate to one's status in other spheres, and how can political equality itself be secured?

HOW TO PROMOTE POLITICAL EQUALITY

In his treatment of the spheres of justice, Walzer argued for ensuring that one's status in each domain support, or at least not undermine, one's status in the other domains. We should seek economic and social policies, for example, that build a foundation for political equality, and as a result, even though we will not find ourselves strictly equal in the economic realm, or even the social one, a rough equality there could support our political equality and permit us to achieve a "complex equality" more generally. But what, precisely, is required of the relations among the three spheres?

Political equality ultimately rests not on the right to vote or the right to hold office but on the rights of association and free expression. It is these rights that support contestation of the status quo, whether that is maintained by the government or by social majorities. The right to contract, meanwhile, is itself also deeply embedded in the right to association. But the moment that societies protect association, expression, and contract, as they must in order to protect human dignity at its most fundamental, they also secure two other phenomena: social discrimination and capitalism. Out of the right of association, socially differentiated groups form, and lines of difference can easily evolve into lines of division and domination. The requirements of political equality, in other words—freedom of association, expression, and contract—generate social phenomena that potentially jeopardize social equality and can lead to economic exploitation.

How, then, can we build institutional frameworks in the social and economic domains that guide our associational practices in the direction of social equality and our economic practices in the direction of egalitarianism? We need a virtuous circle in which political equality supports institutions that, in turn, support social and economic equality—for without those frameworks, the result could well be the emergence of social castes or economic exploitation, either of which would feed back to undermine political equality.

Rising to such a challenge is clearly difficult, but the basic issues involved can be sketched simply. The two fundamental sources of power in a democracy are numbers and control over the state's use of force. The media have access to eyeballs and ears, and therefore to numbers. Wealth, celebrity, and social movement organization can also provide access to eyeballs and ears. Wealth secures that access indirectly, by buying media resources; celebrity brings it directly. Organizing can also achieve such access, but only by dint of hard work. And wealth can also sometimes buy access to institutional control.

Many argue that the most important step needed to restore political equality now is to check the power of money in politics through campaign finance reform or to equalize the resources available to political actors by publicly subsidizing campaigns. They have a point, but by themselves such remedies are insufficient because they focus on only part of the broader picture. Reformers should be considering not merely how to check the power of money in politics but also how to rebuild the power of organizers and organizing as a counterbalance to wealth.

A smart path toward this goal has been identified by the Yale law professor Heather Gerken, who argues for a new federalism that maps out consequential policy domains at all levels of the political system and supports citizen engagement at each level. Gerken's project is not about states' rights; the federal rights enforcement structure would continue to establish the rules of the game for engagement at the local level. But she correctly points out that significant power resides throughout the various layers of U.S. politics and that there are rich egalitarian possibilities in all sorts of areas, from zoning, housing, and transportation to labor markets, education, and regulation. Policy contestation at the local and regional levels, she notes, can drive changes at the national level, with the case of marriage equality being only the most recent prominent example.

Bolstering political equality throughout the lower and middle layers of the U.S. federalized political system is a not an easy or sexy task, but that is what is required to redress the outsize power of money in national life that has been both the consequence and the enabler of rising economic inequality. Liberty and equality can be mutually reinforcing, just as the founders believed. But to make that happen, political equality will need to be secured first and then be used to maintain, and be maintained by, egalitarianism in the social and economic spheres as well.

Danielle Allen is Director of the Edmond J. Safra Center for Ethics at Harvard University and a Professor in Harvard's Department of Government and Graduate School of Education.

Fight or Flight

America's Choice in the Middle East

Kenneth M. Pollack

Houthi fighters patrol the main street of Sadah, Yemen, June 2015.

The modern Middle East has rarely been tranquil, but it has never been this bad. Full-blown civil wars rage in Iraq, Libya, Syria, and Yemen. Nascent conflicts simmer in Egypt, South Sudan, and Turkey. Various forms of spillover from these civil wars threaten the stability of Algeria, Jordan, Lebanon, Saudi Arabia, and Tunisia. Tensions between Iran and Saudi Arabia have risen to new heights, raising the specter of a regionwide religious war. Israel and the Palestinians have experienced a resurgence of low-level violence. Kuwait, Morocco, Oman, Qatar, and the United Arab Emirates have weathered the storm so far, but even they are terrified of what is going on around them. Not since the Mongol invasions of the thirteenth century has the Middle East seen so much chaos.

Moreover, it is unlikely to abate anytime soon. No matter how many times Americans insist that the people of the Middle East will come to their senses and resolve their differences if left to their own devices, they never do. Absent external involvement, the region's leaders consistently opt for strategies that exacerbate conflict and feed perpetual instability. Civil wars are particularly stubborn problems, and without decisive outside intervention, they usually last decades. The Congolese civil war is entering its 22nd year, the Peruvian its 36th, and the Afghan its 37th. There is no reason to expect the Middle East's conflicts to burn out on their own either.

Even as the Middle East careens out of control, help is not on the way.

As a consequence, the next U.S. president is going to face a choice in the Middle East: do much more to stabilize it, or disengage from it much more. But given how tempestuous the region has become, both options—stepping up and stepping back—will cost the United States far more than is typically imagined. Stabilizing the region would almost certainly require more resources, energy, attention, and political capital than most advocates of a forward-leaning U.S. posture recognize. Similarly, giving up more control and abandoning more commitments in the region would require accepting much greater risks than most in this camp acknowledge. The costs of stepping up are more manageable than the risks of stepping back, but either option would be better than muddling through.

MAN, THE STATE, AND CIVIL WAR

Grasping the real choices that the United States faces in the Middle East requires an honest understanding of what is going on there. Although it is fashionable to blame the region's travails on ancient hatreds or the poor cartography of Mr. Sykes and Monsieur Picot, the real problems began with the modern Arab state system. After World War II, the Arab states came into their own. Most shed their European colonial masters, and all adopted more modern political systems, whether secular republics (read: dictatorships) or new monarchies.

None of these states worked very well. For one thing, their economies depended heavily on oil, either directly, by pumping it themselves, or indirectly, via trade, aid, and worker remittances. These rentier economies produced too few jobs and too much wealth that their civilian populations neither controlled nor generated, encouraging the ruling elites to treat their citizenries as (mostly unwanted) dependents. The oil money bred massive corruption, along with bloated public sectors uninterested in the needs or aspirations of the wider populace. To make matters worse, the Arab states had emerged from Ottoman and European colonialism with their traditional sociocultural systems intact, which oil wealth and autocracy made it possible to preserve and even indulge.

An Iraqi soldier in Anbar Province, July 2015.

This model clunked along for several decades, before it started falling apart in the late twentieth century. The oil market became more volatile, with long periods of low prices, which created economic hardship even in oil-rich states such as Algeria, Iraq, and Saudi Arabia. Globalization brought to the region new ideas about the relationship between government and the governed, as well as foreign cultural influences. Arabs (and Iranians, for that matter) increasingly demanded that their governments help fix their problems. But all they got in response was malign neglect.

By the 1990s, popular discontent had risen throughout the Middle East. The Muslim Brotherhood and its many franchises grew quickly as a political opposition to the regimes. Others turned to violence—rioters in the Nejd region of Saudi Arabia, Islamist insurgents in Egypt, and various terrorist groups elsewhere—all seeking to overthrow their governments. Eventually, some of these groups would decide that they first had to drive away the foreign backers of those governments, starting with the United States.

The pent-up frustrations and desire for political change finally exploded in the Arab Spring of 2011, with large-scale protests breaking out in nearly all Arab countries and the toppling or crippling of the regime in five of them. But revolutions are always tricky things to get right. That has proved especially true in the Arab world, where the autocrats in each country had done a superb job of eliminating any charismatic opposition leader who might have unified the country after the fall of the regime and where there were no popular alternative ideas about how to organize a new Arab state. And so in Libya, Syria, and Yemen, the result has been state failure, a security vacuum, and civil war.

The Middle East's travails began with the modern Arab state system.

If the first-order problem of the Middle East is the failure of the postwar Arab state system, the outbreak of civil wars has become an equally important second-order problem. These conflicts have taken on lives of their own, becoming engines of instability that now pose the greatest immediate threat to both the people of the region and the rest of the world.

For one thing, civil wars have a bad habit of spilling over into their neighbors. Vast numbers of refugees cross borders, as do smaller, but no less problematic, numbers of terrorists and other armed combatants. So do ideas promoting militancy, revolution, and secession. In this way, neighboring states can themselves succumb to instability or even internal conflict. Indeed, scholars have found that the strongest predictor that a state will experience a civil war is whether it borders a country already embroiled in one.

Civil wars also have a bad habit of sucking in neighboring countries. Seeking to protect their interests and prevent spillover, states typically choose particular combatants to back. But that brings them into conflict with other neighboring states that have picked their own favorites. Even if this competition remains a proxy fight, it can still be economically and politically draining, even ruinous. At worst, the conflict can lead to a regional war, when a state, convinced its proxy is not doing the job, sends in its own armed forces. For evidence of this dynamic, one need look no further than the Saudi-led intervention in Yemen, or Iranian and Russian military operations in Iraq and Syria.

Soldiers loyal to Syrian President Bashar al-Assad play football in Homs, May 2014.

WITHDRAWAL SYMPTOMS

As if the failure of the postwar Arab state system and the outbreak of four civil wars weren't bad enough, in the midst of all of this, the United States has distanced itself from the region. The Middle East has not been without a great-power overseer of one kind or another since the Ottoman conquests of the sixteenth century. This is not to suggest that the external hegemon was always an unalloyed good; it wasn't. But it often played the constructive role of mitigating conflict. Good or bad, the states of the region have grown accustomed to interacting with one another with a dominating third party in the room, figuratively and often literally.

Disengagement has been most damaging in Iraq. The U.S. withdrawal from the country was the most important of a range of factors that pulled it back into civil war. Scholars have long recognized that shepherding a nation out of a civil war requires some internal or external peacekeeper to guarantee the terms of a new power-sharing arrangement among the warring parties. Over time, that role can become increasingly symbolic, as was the case with NATO in Bosnia. The alliance's presence there dwindled to a militarily insignificant force within about five years, but it still played a crucial political and psychological role in reassuring the rival factions that none of them would return to violence. In the case of Iraq, the United States played that role, and its disengagement in 2010 and 2011 led to exactly what history predicted.

This phenomenon has played out more broadly across the Middle East. The withdrawal of the United States has forced governments there to interact in a novel way, without the hope that Washington will provide a cooperative path out of the security dilemmas that litter the region. U.S. disengagement has made many states fear that others will become more aggressive without the United States to restrain them. That fear has caused them to act more aggressively themselves, which in turn has sparked more severe countermoves, again in the expectation that the United States will not check either the original move or the riposte. This dynamic has grown most acute between Iran and Saudi Arabia, whose tit-for-tat exchange is growing ever more vituperative and violent. The Saudis have taken the stunning step of directly intervening in Yemen's civil war against the country's Houthi minority, which they consider to be an Iranian proxy that threatens their southern flank.

If the next U.S. president is unwilling to commit to stepping up to stabilize the Middle East, the only real alternative is to step back.

Even as the Middle East careens out of control, help is not on the way. The Obama administration's policies toward the region are not designed to mitigate, let alone end, its real problems. That is why the region has gotten worse since President Barack Obama entered office, and why there is no reason to believe that it will get any better before he leaves office.

In his 2009 speech in Cairo, Obama did claim that the United States would try to help the region shift to a new Arab state system, but he never backed his speech up with an actual policy, let alone resources. Then, in 2011, the administration failed to put in place a coherent strategy to deal with the Arab Spring, one that might have assisted a transition to more stable, pluralistic systems of government. Having missed its best opportunities, Washington now barely pays lip service to the need for gradual, long-term reform.

As for the civil wars, the administration has focused on addressing only their symptoms—trying to contain the spillover—by attacking the Islamic State, or ISIS; accepting some refugees; and working to prevent terrorist attacks back home. But the history of civil wars demonstrates that it is extremely hard to contain the spillover, and the Middle East today is proving no exception. Spillover from Syria helped push Iraq back into civil war. In turn, spillover from the Iraqi and Syrian civil wars has generated a low-level civil war in Turkey and threatens to do the same in Jordan and Lebanon. Spillover from Libya is destabilizing Egypt, Mali, and Tunisia.

The Iraqi, Syrian, and Yemeni civil wars have sucked Iran and the Gulf states into a vicious proxy war fought across all three battlefields. And refugees, terrorists, and radicalization spilling over from all these wars have created new dilemmas for Europe and North America.

In fact, it is effectively impossible to eradicate the symptoms of civil wars without treating the underlying maladies. No matter how many thousands of refugees the West accepts, as long as the civil wars grind on, millions more will flee. And no matter how many terrorists the United States kills, without an end to the civil wars, more young men will keep turning to terrorism. Over the past 15 years, the threat from Salafi jihadism has grown by orders of magnitude despite the damage that the United States has inflicted on al Qaeda's core in Afghanistan. In places racked by civil war, the group's offshoots, including ISIS, are finding new recruits, new sanctuaries, and new fields of jihad. But where order prevails, they dissipate. Neither al Qaeda nor ISIS has found much purchase in any of the remaining strong states of the region. And when the United States brought stability to Iraq beginning in 2007, al Qaeda's franchise there was pushed to the brink of extinction, only to find salvation in 2011, when civil war broke out next door in Syria.

Contrary to the conventional wisdom, moreover, it is possible for a third party to settle a civil war long before it might end on its own. Scholars of civil wars have found that in about 20 percent of the cases since 1945, and roughly 40 percent of the cases since 1995, an external actor was able to engineer just such an outcome. Doing so is not easy, of course, but it need not be as ruinously expensive as the United States' painful experience in Iraq.

Ending a civil war requires the intervening power to accomplish three objectives. First, it must change the military dynamics such that none of the warring parties believes that it can win a military victory and none fears that its fighters will be slaughtered once they lay down their arms. Second, it must forge a power-sharing agreement among the various groups so that they all have an equitable stake in a new government. And third, it must put in place institutions that reassure all the parties that the first two conditions will endure. To some extent unknowingly, that is precisely the path NATO followed in Bosnia in 1994–95 and the United States followed in Iraq in 2007–10.

History also shows that when outside powers stray from this approach or commit inadequate resources to it, their interventions inevitably fail and typically make the conflicts bloodier, longer, and less contained. No wonder U.S. policy toward Iraq and Syria (let alone Libya and Yemen) has failed since 2011. And as long as the United States continues to avoid pursuing the one approach that can work, there is no reason to expect anything else. At most, the U.S. military's current campaign against ISIS in Iraq and Syria will engineer the same outcome as its earlier one against al Qaeda in Afghanistan: the United States may badly damage ISIS, but unless it ends the conflicts that sustain it, the group will morph and spread and eventually be succeeded by the son of ISIS, just as ISIS is the son of al Qaeda.

MOHAMED AL-SAYAGHI / REUTERS

A man mourns for relatives killed by an air strike in Sanaa, Yemen, September 2015.

STEPPING UP

Stabilizing the Middle East will require a new approach—one that attacks the root causes of the region's troubles and is backed up by adequate resources. The first priority should be to shut down the current civil wars. In every case, that will require first changing the battlefield dynamics to convince all the warring factions that military victory is impossible. In an ideal world, that would entail sending at least small numbers of U.S. combat forces to Iraq (perhaps 10,000) and potentially Syria. But if the political will for even a modest commitment of forces does not exist, then more advisers, airpower, intelligence sharing, and logistical support could suffice, albeit with a lower likelihood of success.

Regardless, the United States and its allies will also have to build new indigenous militaries able to first defeat the terrorists, militias, and extremists and then serve as the foundation for a new state. In Iraq, that means retraining and reforming the Iraqi security forces to a much greater degree than current U.S. policy envisions. In Libya, Syria, and Yemen, it would mean creating new indigenous, conventional militaries that (with considerable American support) would be able to defeat any potential rival, secure the civilian populaces, and enforce the terms of permanent cease-fires.

In all four civil wars, the United States and its allies will also have to undertake major political efforts aimed at forging equitable power-sharing arrangements. In Iraq, the United States should take the lead in defining both the minimal needs and the potential areas of agreement among the various Shiite and Sunni factions, just as Ryan Crocker, the U.S. ambassador to Iraq in 2007–9, and his team accomplished as part of the U.S. surge strategy. That, plus giving material resources to various moderate Iraqi political leaders and their constituencies among both the Shiites and the Sunnis, should allow the United States to hammer out a new power-sharing deal. Such an arrangement should end the alienation of the Sunni population, which lies at the heart of Iraq's current problems. This, in turn, would make it much easier for the Abadi government and the United States to stand up Sunni military formations to help liberate the Sunni- majority areas of the country from ISIS and help diminish the power of the Iranian-backed Shiite militias.

In Syria, the ongoing peace talks in Vienna provide a starting point for a political solution. But they offer little more than that, because the military conditions are not conducive to a real political compromise, let alone a permanent cessation of hostilities. Neither the Assad regime nor the Western-backed opposition believes that it can afford to stop fighting, and each of the three strongest rebel groups—Ahrar al-Sham, Jabhat al-Nusra, and ISIS—remains convinced that it can achieve total victory. So until the reality on the battlefield shifts, little can be achieved at the negotiating table. If the military situation changes, then Western diplomats should help Syria's communities fashion an arrangement that distributes political power and economic benefits equitably. The deal would have to include the Alawites, but not necessarily President Bashar al-Assad himself, and it would need to assure each faction that the new government would not oppress it, the way the Alawite minority oppressed the Sunni majority in the past.

Stepping back from the Middle East means risking the near- term collapse of Egypt, Jordan, Lebanon, Tunisia, and Turkey.

The turmoil in Libya mirrors that in Syria, except that it is receiving far less international attention. Thus, the first step there is for the United States to convince its partners to take on a more constructive role. If the United States should lead in Iraq and Syria, then Europe needs to lead in Libya. By dint of its economic ties and proximity to Europe, Libya threatens European interests far more directly than it does American ones, and NATO's role in the 2011 intervention in Libya can serve as a precedent for European leadership. Of course, the Europeans will not take on the challenge if they are not convinced that the United States intends to do its part to quell the Middle East's civil wars, further underscoring the importance of a coherent, properly resourced U.S. strategy. To aid Europe's fight in Libya, Washington will undoubtedly have to commit assistance related to logistics, command and control, and intelligence, and possibly even combat advisers.

In Yemen, the Gulf states' air campaign has achieved little, but the intervention by a small ground force led by the United Arab Emirates has set back the rebel coalition, creating a real opportunity to negotiate an end to the conflict. Unfortunately, the Gulf states seem unwilling to offer Yemen's opposition terms that would equitably divide political power and economic benefits, and they seem equally unwilling to offer security guarantees. To draw the conflict to a close, the United States and its allies will have to encourage their partners in the Gulf to make meaningful concessions. If that doesn't work, then the most useful thing they can do is try to convince the Gulf states to minimize their involvement in Yemen before the strain of intervention threatens their own internal cohesion.

After ending the current civil wars, the next priority of a stepped-up U.S. strategy in the Middle East will be to shore up the states in the greatest danger of sliding into future civil wars: Egypt, Jordan, Tunisia, and Turkey. It is state failure—not external attack by ISIS, al Qaeda, or Iranian proxies—that represents the true source of the conflicts roiling the Middle East today. These four at-risk countries are all badly in need of economic assistance and infrastructure development. But above all, they need political reform to avoid state failure. Consequently, the United States and its allies should offer a range of trade benefits, financial incentives, and economic aid in return for gradual but concrete steps toward political reform. Here, the aim need not be democratization per se (although Tunisia should be strongly encouraged to continue down that path), but it should be good governance, in the form of justice and the rule of law, transparency, and a fair distribution of public goods and services.

The final piece of the puzzle is to press for reform more broadly across the Middle East—economic, social, and political. Even if the United States and its allies succeed in resolving today's civil wars, unless a new state system takes the place of the failed postwar one, the same old problems will recur. Reform will be a hard sell for the region's leaders, who have long resisted it out of a fear that it would strip them of their power and positions. Paradoxically, however, the civil wars may furnish a solution to this conundrum. All the states of the region are terrified of the spillover from these conflicts, and they are desperate for U.S. help in eliminating the threat. In particular, many of the United States' Arab allies have grown frustrated by the gains that Iran has made by exploiting power vacuums. Just as the United States and its allies should offer the region's fragile states economic assistance in return for reform, so they should condition their efforts to end the civil wars on the willingness of the region's stronger states to embrace similar reforms.

STEPPING BACK

If the next U.S. president is unwilling to commit to stepping up to stabilize the Middle East, the only real alternative is to step back from it. Because civil wars do not lend themselves to anything but the right strategy with the right resources, trying the wrong one means throwing U.S. resources away on a lost cause. It probably also means making the situation worse, not better. Under a policy of real disengagement, the United States would abstain from involvement in the civil wars altogether. It would instead try to contain their spillover, difficult as that is, and if that were to fail, it would fall back on defending only core U.S. interests in the Middle East.

The Obama administration has done a creditable job of bolstering Jordan against chaos from Iraq and Syria so far, and stepping back from the region could still entail beefing up U.S. support to Jordan and other at-risk neighbors of the civil wars, such as Egypt, Lebanon, Tunisia, and Turkey. All these countries want and need Western economic, diplomatic, technical, and military assistance. But because spillover has historically proved so difficult to contain, there is a high risk that one or more of them could still slide into civil war themselves, generating yet more spillover.

A civilian inspects a site that was hit by an Israeli strike in Damascus, December 2015.

For that reason, stepping back would also require Washington to make a ruthless assessment of what is the least the United States can do to secure its vital interests in the Middle East. And although it may be a gross exaggeration to say so, in large part, U.S. interests in the region do ultimately come down to Israel, terrorism, and oil.

As poll after poll has found, a majority of Americans continue to see the safety of Israel as important to them and to the United States. Yet Israel today is as safe as the United States can make it. Israeli forces can defeat any conventional foe and deter any deterrable unconventional threat. The United States has defended Israel diplomatically and militarily countless times, including implicitly threatening the Soviet Union with nuclear war during the 1973 Yom Kippur War. The United States has even taken an Iranian nuclear threat off the table for at least the next decade, thanks to the deal it brokered last year. The only threat the United States cannot save Israel from is its own chronic civil war with the Palestinians, but the best solution to that conflict is a peace settlement that neither the Israelis nor the Palestinians have demonstrated much interest in. In short, there is little more that Israel needs from the United States for its own direct security, and what it does need (such as arms sales) the United States could easily provide even if it stepped back from the Middle East.

Perhaps the greatest advantage of a reduced U.S. presence in the Middle East is that it should mitigate the threat from terrorism. Terrorists from the region attack Americans largely because they feel aggrieved by U.S. policies, just as they attack France and the United Kingdom because those countries are staunch U.S. allies (and former colonial powers) and have started to attack Russia because it has intervened in Syria. The less the United States is involved in the Middle East, the less its people are likely to be attacked by terrorists from the region. It is no accident that Switzerland does not suffer from Middle Eastern terrorism.

Of course, even if Washington disengaged from the region as much as possible, Americans would not be entirely immune from Middle Eastern terrorism. The region's conspiracy- mongers endlessly blame the United States for things it didn't do, as well as for what it did, and so terrorists could still find reasons to target Americans. Besides, even under this minimalist approach, the United States would maintain its support for Israel and Saudi Arabia, both of which a range of terrorist groups detest.

If U.S. interests concerning Israel and terrorism would largely take care of themselves in the event that Washington further diminished its role in the Middle East, the same cannot be said for the flow of oil. The idea that fracking has granted the United States energy independence is a myth; as long as the global economy relies on fossil fuels, the United States will be vulnerable to major disruptions in the supply of oil, regardless of how much it produces. Since neither global dependence on oil nor the Middle East's contribution to the share of global production is expected to abate over the next 25 years, the United States will continue to have a critical interest in keeping Middle Eastern oil flowing.

Yet the United States need not defend every last barrel of oil in the region. The question is, how much is enough? This is where things get complicated. Many countries possess strategic reserves of oil that can mitigate a sudden, unexpected drop in production. And some, particularly Saudi Arabia, have enough excess capacity to pump and export more oil if need be. Fracking, likewise, allows North American producers of shale oil to partly compensate for shortfalls. Even though oil production in Libya has dropped by over 80 percent since 2011 as a result of its civil war, other producers have been able to make up for the loss.

Saudi Arabia, however, is in a category of its own. The country produces over ten percent of all the oil used in the world and contains the vast majority of excess capacity; even if every country emptied its strategic oil reserves and fracked like crazy, that would still not compensate for the loss of Saudi oil production. Thus, the United States will have to continue to protect its Saudi allies. But against what? No Middle Eastern state (even Iran) has the capacity to conquer Saudi Arabia, and the modest U.S. air and naval force currently in the Persian Gulf is more than adequate to defeat an Iranian attack on the country's oil infrastructure.

The kingdom's principal threats are internal. Although no one has ever made money betting against the House of Saud, the monarchy rules over a quintessentially dysfunctional postwar Arab state, one that faces daunting political, economic, and social stresses. The Shiites who make up the majority of Saudi Arabia's oil-rich Eastern Province have rioted and resisted government oppression for decades, and their unhappiness has grown with the widening Shiite-Sunni rift across the region. The kingdom skated through the Arab Spring primarily thanks to the far-reaching (if gradual) reform program of King Abdullah, coupled with massive cash payoffs to the people. But Abdullah died in January 2015, and his successor, King Salman, has yet to demonstrate a similar commitment to reform. Even as oil prices remain low, Salman is spending profligately at home and abroad (including on the expensive intervention in Yemen), burning through the kingdom's sovereign wealth fund at $12–$14 billion per month. At that rate, the fund will be empty in about four years, but the king will probably face domestic challenges long before then.

How can the United States protect Saudi Arabia from itself? It is impossible to imagine any U.S. president deploying troops there to suppress a popular revolution or to hold together a failing monarchy. Moreover, the longer that civil wars burn on Saudi Arabia's northern border, in Iraq, and southern border, in Yemen, the more likely these conflicts will destabilize the kingdom—to say nothing of the possibility of a Jordanian civil war. But a strategy of stepping back from the region means the United States will not try to shut down the nearby civil wars, and Washington has little leverage it can use to convince the Saudis to reform. It would have especially little leverage if it swore off the only thing that the Saudis truly want: greater U.S. involvement to end the civil wars and prevent Iran from exploiting them. In these circumstances, the United States would have virtually no ability to save Saudi Arabia from itself if its rulers were to insist on following a ruinous path. Yet in the context of greater U.S. disengagement, that is the most likely course the Saudis would take.

NO EXIT

Ultimately, the greatest challenge for the United States if it steps back from the Middle East is this: figuring out how to defend U.S. interests when they are threatened by problems the United States is ill equipped to solve. Because containing the spillover from civil wars is so difficult, stepping back means risking the near-term collapse of

Egypt, Jordan, Lebanon, Tunisia, and Turkey. Although none of these countries produces much oil itself, their instability could spread to the oil producers, too, over the longer term. The world might be able to survive the loss of Iranian, Iraqi, Kuwaiti, or Algerian oil production, but at a certain point, the instability would affect Saudi Arabia. And even if it never does, it is not clear that the world can afford to lose several lesser oil producers, either.

The great benefit of a policy of stepping back is that it would drastically reduce the burden that the United States would have to bear to stabilize the Middle East. The great danger, however, is that it would entail enormous risks. Once the United States started writing off countries—shortening the list of those it would defend against threats—it is unclear where it would be able to stop, and retreat could turn into rout. If Jordan or Kuwait slid into civil war, would the United States deploy 100,000 troops to occupy and stabilize either country to protect Saudi Arabia (and in the case of civil war in Jordan, to protect Israel)? Could the United States do so in time to prevent the spillover from destabilizing the kingdom? If not, are there other ways to keep the kingdom itself from falling? Given all these uncertainties, the most prudent course is for Americans to steel themselves against the costs and step up to stabilize the region.

That said, what the United States should certainly not do is refuse to choose between stepping up and stepping back and instead waffle somewhere in the middle, committing enough resources to enlarge its burden without increasing the likelihood that its moves will make anything better. Civil wars do not lend themselves to half measures. An outside power has to do the right thing and pay the attendant costs, or else its intervention will only make the situation worse for everyone involved, including itself. The tragedy is that given the U.S. political system's tendency to avoid decisive moves, the next administration will almost inevitably opt to muddle through. Given the extent of the chaos in the Middle East today, refusing to choose would likely prove to be the worst choice of all.

KENNETH M. POLLACK is a Senior Fellow at the Brookings Institution.

© Foreign Affairs

Russia's Perpetual Geopolitics

Putin Returns to the Historical Pattern

Stephen Kotkin

Follow the leader: Peter the Great by Hippolyte (Paul) Delaroche, 1838.

For half a millennium, Russian foreign policy has been characterized by soaring ambitions that have exceeded the country's capabilities. Beginning with the reign of Ivan the Terrible in the sixteenth century, Russia managed to expand at an average rate of 50 square miles per day for hundreds of years, eventually covering one-sixth of the earth's landmass. By 1900, it was the world's fourth- or fifth-largest industrial power and the largest agricultural producer in Europe. But its per capita GDP reached only 20 percent of the United Kingdom's and 40 percent of Germany's. Imperial Russia's average life span at birth was just 30 years—higher than British India's (23) but the same as Qing China's and far below the United Kingdom's (52), Japan's (51), and Germany's (49). Russian literacy in the early twentieth century remained below 33 percent—lower than that of Great Britain in the eighteenth century. These comparisons were all well known by the Russian political establishment, because its members traveled to Europe frequently and measured their country against the world's leaders (something that is true today, as well).

History records three fleeting moments of remarkable Russian ascendancy: Peter the Great's victory over Charles XII and a declining Sweden in the early 1700s, which implanted Russian power on the Baltic Sea and in Europe; Alexander I's victory over a wildly overstretched Napoleon in the second decade of the nineteenth century, which brought Russia to Paris as an arbiter of great-power affairs; and Stalin's victory over the maniacal gambler Adolf Hitler in the 1940s, which gained Russia Berlin, a satellite empire in Eastern Europe, and a central role shaping the global postwar order.

These high-water marks aside, however, Russia has almost always been a relatively weak great power. It lost the Crimean War of 1853–56, a defeat that ended the post-Napoleonic glow and forced a belated emancipation of the serfs. It lost the Russo-Japanese War of 1904–5, the first defeat of a European country by an Asian one in the modern era. It lost World War I, a defeat that caused the collapse of the imperial regime. And it lost the Cold War, a defeat that helped cause the collapse of the imperial regime's Soviet successor.

Throughout, the country has been haunted by its relative backwardness, particularly in the military and industrial spheres. This has led to repeated frenzies of government activity designed to help the country catch up, with a familiar cycle of coercive state-led industrial growth followed by stagnation. Most analysts had assumed that this pattern had ended for good in the 1990s, with the abandonment of Marxism-Leninism and the arrival of competitive elections and a buccaneer capitalist economy. But the impetus behind Russian grand strategy had not changed. And over the last decade, Russian President Vladimir Putin has returned to the trend of relying on the state to manage the gulf between Russia and the more powerful West.

Russian foreign policy has long been characterized by soaring ambitions that have exceeded the country's capabilities.

With the breakup of the Soviet Union in 1991, Moscow lost some two million square miles of sovereign territory—more than the equivalent of the entire European Union (1.7 million square miles) or India (1.3 million). Russia forfeited the share of Germany it had conquered in World War II and its other satellites in Eastern Europe—all of which are now inside the Western military alliance, along with some advanced former regions of the Soviet Union, such as the Baltic states. Other former Soviet possessions, such as Azerbaijan, Georgia, and Ukraine, cooperate closely with the West on security matters. Notwithstanding the forcible annexation of Crimea, the war in eastern Ukraine, and the de facto occupation of Abkhazia and South Ossetia, Russia has had to retreat from most of Catherine the Great's so-called New Russia, in the southern steppes, and from Transcaucasia. And apart from a few military bases, Russia is out of Central Asia, too.

Russia is still the largest country in the world, but it is much smaller than it was, and the extent of a country's territory matters less for great-power status these days than economic dynamism and human capital—spheres in which Russia has also declined. Russian dollar-denominated GDP peaked in 2013 at slightly more than $2 trillion and has now dropped to about $1.2 trillion thanks to cratering oil prices and ruble exchange rates. To be sure, the contraction measured in purchasing power parity has been far less dramatic. But in comparative dollar-denominated terms, Russia's economy amounts to a mere 1.5 percent of global GDP and is just one-15th the size of the U.S. economy. Russia also suffers the dubious distinction of being the most corrupt developed country in the world, and its resource-extracting, rent-seeking economic system has reached a dead end.

The geopolitical environment, meanwhile, has become only more challenging over time, with continuing U.S. global supremacy and the dramatic rise of China. And the spread of radical political Islam poses concerns, as about 15 percent of Russia's 142 million citizens are Muslim and some of the country's predominantly Muslim regions are seething with unrest and lawlessness. For Russian elites who assume that their country's status and even survival depend on matching the West, the limits of the current course should be evident.

THE BEAR'S NECESSITIES

Russians have always had an abiding sense of living in a providential country with a special mission—an attitude often traced to Byzantium, which Russia claims as an inheritance. In truth, most great powers have exhibited similar feelings. Both China and the United States have claimed a heavenly mandated exceptionalism, as did England and France throughout much of their histories. Germany and Japan had their exceptionalism bombed out of them. Russia's is remarkably resilient. It has been expressed differently over time—the Third Rome, the pan-Slavic kingdom, the world headquarters of the Communist International. Today's version involves Eurasianism, a movement launched among Russian émigrés in 1921 that imagined Russia as neither European nor Asian but a sui generis fusion.

The sense of having a special mission has contributed to Russia's paucity of formal alliances and reluctance to join international bodies except as an exceptional or dominant member. It furnishes Russia's people and leaders with pride, but it also fuels resentment toward the West for supposedly underappreciating Russia's uniqueness and importance. Thus is psychological alienation added to the institutional divergence driven by relative economic backwardness. As a result, Russian governments have generally oscillated between seeking closer ties with the West and recoiling in fury at perceived slights, with neither tendency able to prevail permanently.

EDUARD KORNIYENKO / REUTERS

Children, wearing red neckerchiefs, a symbol of the Pioneer Organization, attend a ceremony for the inauguration of new members at a school in Stavropol region, Russia, November 2015.

Yet another factor that has shaped Russia's role in the world has been the country's unique geography. It has no natural borders, except the Pacific Ocean and the Arctic Ocean (the latter of which is now becoming a contested space, too). Buffeted throughout its history by often turbulent developments in East Asia, Europe, and the Middle East, Russia has felt perennially vulnerable and has often displayed a kind of defensive aggressiveness. Whatever the original causes behind early Russian expansionism—much of which was unplanned—many in the country's political class came to believe over time that only further expansion could secure the earlier acquisitions. Russian security has thus traditionally been partly predicated on moving outward, in the name of preempting external attack.

Today, too, smaller countries on Russia's borders are viewed less as potential friends than as potential beachheads for enemies. In fact, this sentiment was strengthened by the Soviet collapse. Unlike Stalin, Putin does not recognize the existence of a Ukrainian nation separate from a Russian one. But like Stalin, he views all nominally independent borderland states, now including Ukraine, as weapons in the hands of Western powers intent on wielding them against Russia.

Russia is the most corrupt developed country in the world, and its resource-extracting, rent-seeking economic system has reached a dead end.

A final driver of Russian foreign policy has been the country's perennial quest for a strong state. In a dangerous world with few natural defenses, the thinking runs, the only guarantor of Russia's security is a powerful state willing and able to act aggressively in its own interests. A strong state has also been seen as the guarantor of domestic order, and the result has been a trend captured in the nineteenth-century historian Vasily Klyuchevsky's one-line summation of a millennium of Russian history: "The state grew fat, but the people grew lean."

Paradoxically, however, the efforts to build a strong state have invariably led to subverted institutions and personalistic rule. Peter the Great, the original strong-state builder, emasculated individual initiative, exacerbated inbred distrust among officials, and fortified patron-client tendencies. His coercive modernization brought indispensable new industries, but his project for a strengthened state actually entrenched personal whim. This syndrome characterized the reigns of successive Romanov autocrats and those of Lenin and, especially, Stalin, and it has persisted to this day. Unbridled personalism tends to render decision-making on Russian grand strategy opaque and potentially capricious, for it ends up conflating state interests with the political fortunes of one person.

MUST THE PAST BE PROLOGUE?

Anti-Western resentment and Russian patriotism appear particularly pronounced in Putin's personality and life experiences, but a different Russian government not run by former KGB types would still be confronted with the challenge of weakness vis-à-vis the West and the desire for a special role in the world. Russia's foreign policy orientation, in other words, is as much a condition as a choice. But if Russian elites could somehow redefine their sense of exceptionalism and put aside their unwinnable competition with the West, they could set their country on a less costly, more promising course.

Russian governments have generally oscillated between seeking closer ties with the West and recoiling in fury at perceived slights.

Superficially, this appeared to be what was happening during the 1990s, before Putin took the helm, and in Russia a powerful "stab in the back" story has taken shape about how it was an arrogant West that spurned Russian overtures over the last couple of decades rather than the reverse. But such a view downplays the dynamic inside Russia. Certainly, Washington exploited Russia's enfeeblement during the tenure of Russian President Boris Yeltsin and beyond. But it is not necessary to have supported every aspect of Western policy in recent decades to see Putin's evolving stance less as a reaction to external moves than as the latest example of a deep, recurring pattern driven by internal factors. What precluded post-Soviet Russia from joining Europe as just another country or forming an (inevitably) unequal partnership with the United States was the country's abiding great-power pride and sense of special mission. Until Russia brings its aspirations into line with its actual capabilities, it cannot become a "normal" country, no matter what the rise in its per capita GDP or other quantitative indicators is.

GLEB GARANICH / REUTERS

A boy sits on a swing near his building, which was damaged during fighting between the Ukrainian army and pro-Russian separatists, next to a Ukrainian armored personnel carrier, near Donetsk, eastern Ukraine, June 2015.

Let's be clear: Russia is a remarkable civilization of tremendous depth. It is not the only former absolute monarchy that has had trouble attaining political stability or that retains a statist bent (think of France, for example). And Russia is right in thinking that the post–Cold War settlement was unbalanced, even unfair. But that was not because of any intentional humiliation or betrayal. It was the inevitable result of the West's decisive victory in the contest with the Soviet Union. In a multidimensional global rivalry—political, economic, cultural, technological, and military—the Soviet Union lost across the board. Mikhail Gorbachev's Kremlin chose to bow out gracefully rather than pull the world down along with it, but that extraordinarily benevolent endgame did not change the nature of the outcome or its causes—something that post-Soviet Russia has never really accepted.

The outside world cannot force such a psychological recognition, what the Germans call Vergangenheitsbewältigung—"coming to terms with the past." But there is no reason it could not come about organically, among Russians themselves. Eventually, the country could try to follow something like the trajectory of France, which retains a lingering sense of exceptionalism yet has made peace with its loss of its external empire and its special mission in the world, recalibrating its national idea to fit its reduced role and joining with lesser powers and small countries in Europe on terms of equality.

Whether even a transformed Russia would be accepted into and merge well with Europe is an open question. But the start of the process would need to be a Russian leadership able to get its public to accept permanent retrenchment and agree to embark on an arduous domestic restructuring. Outsiders should be humble as they contemplate how wrenching such an adjustment would be, especially without a hot-war defeat and military occupation.

It took France and the United Kingdom decades to relinquish their own senses of exceptionalism and global responsibility, and some would argue that their elites have still not fully done so. But even they have high GDPs, top-rated universities, financial power, and global languages. Russia has none of that. It does possess a permanent veto in the UN Security Council, as well as one of the world's two foremost doomsday arsenals and world-class cyberwarfare capabilities. These, plus its unique geography, do give it a kind of global reach. And yet, Russia is living proof that hard power is brittle without the other dimensions of great-power status. However much Russia might insist on being acknowledged as an equal to the United States, the European Union, or even China, it is not, and it has no near- or medium-term prospect of becoming one.

AND NOW FOR SOMETHING COMPLETELY DIFFERENT

What are Russia's concrete alternatives to a European-style restructuring and orientation? It has a very long history of being on the Pacific—and failing to become an Asian power. What it can claim is predominance in its region. There is no match for its conventional military among the other Soviet successor states, and the latter (with the exception of the Baltic states) are also economically dependent on Russia to various degrees. But regional military supremacy and economic leverage in Eurasia cannot underwrite enduring great-power status. Putin has failed to make the Eurasian Economic Union successful—but even if all potential members joined and worked together, their combined economic capabilities would still be relatively small.

Until Russia brings its aspirations into line with its actual capabilities, it cannot become a "normal" country.

Russia is a big market, and that can be attractive, but neighboring countries see risks as well as rewards in bilateral trade with the country. Estonia, Georgia, and Ukraine, for example, are generally willing to do business with Russia only provided they have an anchor in the West. Other states that are more economically dependent on Russia, such as Belarus and Kazakhstan, see risks in partnering with a country that not only lacks a model for sustained development but also, in the wake of its annexation of Crimea, might have territorial designs on them. A ballyhooed "strategic partnership" with China, meanwhile, has predictably produced little Chinese financing or investment to compensate for Western sanctions. And all the while, China has openly and vigorously been building its own Greater Eurasia, from the South China Sea through inner Asia to Europe, at Russia's expense and with its cooperation.

Today's muscular Russia is actually in structural decline, and Putin's actions have unwittingly yielded a Ukraine more ethnically homogeneous and more Western-oriented than ever before. Moscow has tense relations with nearly every one of its neighbors and even with its biggest trading partners, including most recently Turkey. Even Germany, Russia's most important foreign policy counterpart and one of its most important economic partners, has had enough, backing sanctions at a cost to its own domestic situation.

"It looks like the so-called 'winners' of the Cold War are determined to have it all and reshape the world into a place that could better serve their interests alone," Putin lectured the annual Valdai Discussion Club gathering in October 2014, following his Crimean annexation. But what poses an existential threat to Russia is not NATO or the West but Russia's own regime. Putin helped rescue the Russian state but has put it back on a trajectory of stagnation and even possible failure. The president and his clique have repeatedly announced the dire necessity of prioritizing economic and human development, yet they shrink from the far-reaching internal restructuring necessary to make that happen, instead pouring resources into military modernization. What Russia really needs to compete effectively and secure a stable place in the international order is transparent, competent, and accountable government; a real civil service; a genuine parliament; a professional and impartial judiciary; free and professional media; and a vigorous, nonpolitical crackdown on corruption.

HOW TO AVOID BEARBAITING

Russia's current leadership continues to make the country bear the burdens of a truculent and independent foreign policy that is beyond the country's means and has produced few positive results. The temporary high afforded by a cunning and ruthless policy in Syria's civil war should not obscure the severity of Russia's recurrent strategic bind—one in which weakness and grandeur combine to produce an autocrat who tries to leap forward by concentrating power, which results in a worsening of the very strategic dilemma he is supposed to be solving. What are the implications of this for Western policy? How should Washington manage relations with a nuclear- and cyber-armed country whose rulers seek to restore its lost dominance, albeit a lesser version; undercut European unity; and make the country "relevant," come what may?

In this context, it is useful to recognize that there has actually never been a period of sustained good relations between Russia and the United States. (Declassified documents reveal that even the World War II alliance was fraught with deeper distrust and greater cross-purposes than has generally been understood.) This has been due not to misunderstandings, miscommunication, or hurt feelings but rather to divergent fundamental values and state interests, as each country has defined them. For Russia, the highest value is the state; for the United States, it is individual liberty, private property, and human rights, usually set out in opposition to the state. So expectations should be kept in check. Equally important, the United States should neither exaggerate the Russian threat nor underplay its own many advantages.

Russia today is not a revolutionary power threatening to overthrow the international order. Moscow operates within a familiar great-power school of international relations, one that prioritizes room for maneuver over morality and assumes the inevitability of conflict, the supremacy of hard power, and the cynicism of others' motives. In certain places and on certain issues, Russia has the ability to thwart U.S. interests, but it does not even remotely approach the scale of the threat posed by the Soviet Union, so there is no need to respond to it with a new Cold War.

The real challenge today boils down to Moscow's desire for Western recognition of a Russian sphere of influence in the former Soviet space (with the exception of the Baltic states). This is the price for reaching accommodation with Putin—something advocates of such accommodation do not always acknowledge frankly. It was the sticking point that prevented enduring cooperation after 9/11, and it remains a concession the West should never grant. Neither, however, is the West really able to protect the territorial integrity of the states inside Moscow's desired sphere of influence. And bluffing will not work. So what should be done?

There has actually never been a period of sustained good relations between Russia and the United States.

Some invoke George Kennan and call for a revival of containment, arguing that external pressure will keep Russia at bay until its authoritarian regime liberalizes or collapses. And certainly, many of Kennan's insights remain pertinent, such as his emphasis in the "Long Telegram" that he dispatched from Moscow 70 years ago on the deep insecurity that drove Soviet behavior. Adopting his thinking now would entail maintaining or intensifying sanctions in response to Russian violations of international law, shoring up Western alliances politically, and upgrading NATO's military readiness. But a new containment could become a trap, re- elevating Russia to the status of rival superpower, Russia's quest for which has helped bring about the current confrontation.

Once again, patient resolve is the key. It is not clear how long Russia can play its weak hand in opposition to the United States and the EU, frightening its neighbors, alienating its most important trading partners, ravaging its own business climate, and hemorrhaging talent. At some point, feelers will be put out for some sort of rapprochement, just as sanctions fatigue will eventually kick in, creating the possibility for some sort of deal. That said, it is also possible that the present standoff might not end anytime soon, since Russia's pursuit of a Eurasian sphere of influence is a matter of national identity not readily susceptible to material cost- benefit calculations.

The trick will be to hold a firm line when necessary—such as refusing to recognize a privileged Russian sphere even when Moscow is able to enact one militarily—while offering negotiations only from a position of strength and avoiding stumbling into unnecessary and counterproductive confrontations on most other issues. Someday, Russia's leaders may come to terms with the glaring limits of standing up to the West and seeking to dominate Eurasia. Until then, Russia will remain not another necessary crusade to be won but a problem to be managed.

STEPHEN KOTKIN is Professor of History and International Affairs at Princeton University and a Fellow at the Hoover Institution at Stanford University.

Making America Great Again

The Case for the Mixed Economy

Jacob S. Hacker and Paul Pierson

Shovel ready: a federally funded road project in Colorado, May 2009.

At a debate among the Republican presidential candidates in March, U.S. Senator Ted Cruz of Texas boiled down his campaign message to its essentials: "Here's my philosophy. The less government, the more freedom. The fewer bureaucrats, the more prosperity. And there are bureaucrats in Washington right now who are killing jobs and I'll tell you, I know who they are. I will find them and I will fire them."

What was remarkable about this statement was how unremarkable it was. Cruz was not taking a radical position; he was expressing his party's orthodoxy, using boilerplate language to signal that he understood the conservative movement's core concerns. For years, his fellow Republicans have taken comparable stands. When Texas Governor

Rick Perry got into trouble while making a similar pledge in a presidential candidate debate in 2011, for example, it was not because he promised to eliminate several federal agencies—Cruz wants to eliminate even more—but because he couldn't remember all the particular agencies he wanted to jettison.

Even if the candidates making them are elected, specific promises about, say, closing major government agencies are bound to be broken, for reasons of simple practicality. As a debate moderator had pointed out to Cruz a few weeks earlier, for example, once he had eliminated the Internal Revenue Service, there would be nobody left to see that taxes were collected, which would pose something of a problem for the functioning of the government. But the spread of this sort of thinking in recent decades has had important effects nonetheless, contributing to increased hostility to government and a major retrenchment in government activities.

Many conservatives complain that this contraction has been too limited and that cutting back even further would unleash powerful forces in the U.S. economy and society that would help solve problems such as slow growth, stagnating incomes, low labor-force participation, and rising inequality. They tell a story about a bygone era of economic dynamism when men and markets were free—a laissez-faire Eden that was lost when progressive politicians such as Woodrow Wilson started using government power to try to "improve" things and ushered in a century of increasingly tyrannical government meddling that has led to a host of terrible outcomes.

The truth is almost precisely the opposite. The spread of capitalism in the eighteenth and nineteenth centuries triggered innovation, growth, and economic progress, but so long as markets were relatively unconstrained, the scale and benefits of that economic dynamism were often limited, inconsistently delivered, unequally distributed, and too frequently unfairly captured by powerful private actors. It was the emergence in the first half of the twentieth century of a robust U.S. government willing and able to act boldly on behalf of the country as a whole that led to spectacular advances in national well-being over many decades—and it has been the withering of government capabilities, ambitions, and independence in the last generation or two that has been a major cause of the drying up of the good times.

There has been nothing inevitable about the trend toward weaker, less functional government; it has been driven by a relentless campaign over many decades to delegitimize the stronger U.S. government that did so much good earlier in the century. So the trend can be reversed. But it will take an equally persistent campaign in the opposite direction, devoted to reminding Americans of what they once understood so well: that a government capable of rising above narrow private interests and supporting broader public concerns is part of the solution, not the problem.

WHAT ADAM SMITH UNDERSTOOD

Like other advanced democratic nations, the United States has what economists call a "mixed economy." In this public- private arrangement, markets play the dominant role in producing and allocating goods and innovating to meet consumer demand. Visionaries such as Apple's Steve Jobs see untapped opportunities to make money by satisfying human wants and then draw on the knowledge and technology around them to produce goods and services for which people are willing to pay. Alongside companies such as Apple, however, government plays a dominant or vital role in the many areas where markets fall short. As the economist Mariana Mazzucato has documented, if you look inside that iPhone, you'll find that most of its major components (GPS, lithium-ion batteries, cellular technology, touch-screen and lcd displays, Internet connectivity) rest on research that was publicly funded or even directly carried out by government agencies.

Jobs and his creative team transformed all of this into something uniquely valuable. But they couldn't have done it without the U.S. government's huge investments in technical knowledge—knowledge that all companies can use and thus none has a strong incentive to produce. That knowledge is embodied not just in science and technology but also in a skilled work force that government fosters directly and indirectly: through K–12 schools, loans for higher education, and the provision of social supports that encourage beneficial risk taking. And even if government had played no role in seeding or enabling Apple's products, it would still be responsible for much of the economic and physical infrastructure—from national monetary policy to local roads—on which the California tech giant relies.

Of course, affluent democracies differ in the exact form that this public-private mix takes, and not all mixes are equally effective. Public policies don't always foster prosperity. Those within government can hurt, rather than harness, the market, distributing favors to narrow interest groups or constraining economic dynamism in ways that stifle growth. No less important (though more neglected), they can fail to respond to problems in the market that could and should be addressed by effective public action, hindering growth through omission rather than commission. For all of this, however, no country has risen to broad prosperity without complementing private markets with an extensive array of core functions that rest on public authority—without, that is, a mixed economy.

That markets fall short under certain conditions has been known for centuries. In the eighteenth century, Adam Smith wrote enthusiastically about the "invisible hand" of market allocation. Yet he also identified many cases in which rational actors pursuing their own self-interest produced bad outcomes: underinvestment in education, financial instability, insufficient infrastructure, unchecked monopolies. Economists have been building on these insights ever since to explain when and why markets stumble and how the visible hand of government can make the invisible hand more effective.

Democracy and the market have to work together, but they also need to be partly independent from each other.

The visible hand is needed, for example, to provide collective goods that markets won't, such as education, infrastructure, courts, and basic scientific research; to reduce negative spillover costs that market participants don't bear fully, such as pollution; to encourage positive spillover benefits that such parties don't take fully into account, such as valuable shared knowledge; to regulate the market to protect consumers and investors from corporate predation and from their own myopic behavior; to provide or require insurance against medical and retirement costs; and to soften the business cycle and reduce the risk of financial crises.

The political economist Charles Lindblom once described markets as being like fingers: nimble and dexterous. Governments, with their capacity to exercise authority, are like thumbs: powerful but lacking subtlety and flexibility. The invisible hand is all fingers. The visible hand is all thumbs. One wouldn't want to be all thumbs, of course, but one wouldn't want to be all fingers, either. Thumbs provide countervailing power, constraint, and adjustment to get the best out of those nimble fingers.

To achieve this potential requires not just an appropriate division of labor but also a healthy balance of power. Markets give rise to resourceful economic actors who want government to favor them. Absent measures to blunt their political edge, their demands will drown out the voices of consumers, workers, and concerned citizens.

Today, most of the discussion of the political power of market actors suggests that such "crony capitalism" can be avoided simply by reducing governance to a bare minimum. As Smith clearly recognized, however, the intermingling of markets and politics is inevitable: a private sector completely free of government influence is just as mythical (and undesirable) as a government completely free of private-sector influence. And a government that doesn't act in the face of distorted markets is imposing costs on society as a whole that are just as real as those imposed when a government acts in favor of narrow claimants. Trying to reduce rent seeking by crippling active government means embracing a cure far worse than the original disease.

Snowplow trucks work on the roads as snow falls in Washington, D.C., January 2016.

The mixed economy, in short, solves a major dilemma. The private markets that generally foster prosperity routinely fail, sometimes spectacularly so. At the same time, the government policies that are needed to respond to these failures are perpetually under siege from the very market players that help fuel growth. Democracy and the market have to work together, but they also need to be partly independent from each other, or the thumb will cease to apply effective counterpressure to the fingers. Smith recognized this dilemma, but it was never resolved adequately during his lifetime, in part because neither markets nor democracies had achieved the scale and sophistication necessary to make broad prosperity possible. In the twentieth century, that changed.

CROSSING THE GREAT DIVIDE

The mixed economy is a social institution, a human solution to human problems. Private capitalism and public coercion each predated modern prosperity. What was new was the marriage of large-scale profit-seeking activity, active democratic governance, and a deepened understanding of how markets work (and when they work poorly).

As in any marriage, the exact terms of the relationship changed over time. In an evolving world, social institutions need to adapt if they are to continue to serve their basic functions. Money, for example, is still doing what it has always done: providing a common metric, storing value, and facilitating exchange. But it's now paper or plastic rather than metal and more likely to pass from computer to computer than hand to hand. Similarly, the mixed economy is defined not by the specific forms it has taken but by the specific functions it has served: overcoming market failures and translating economic growth into broad advances in human well-being.

The effective performance of these functions has delivered truly miraculous breakthroughs. Indeed, the mixed economy may well be the greatest invention in history. It is also a strikingly recent invention. Plot the growth of Western economies on an axis against the passage of time, and the line would be mostly flat for thousands of years. Even the emergence of capitalism, momentous as it was, was not synonymous with the birth of mass prosperity. Trapped in a Malthusian race between population and sustenance, societies remained on the brink of destitution until well into the nineteenth century. Life expectancy rose only modestly between the Neolithic Period, about 10,000 BC to 3500 BC, and the Victorian era, 1837 to 1901. An American born in the late nineteenth century had an average life expectancy of around 45 years, and a large share of Americans never made it past their first birthdays.

Then something remarkable happened. In countries on the frontier of economic development, human health began to improve rapidly, educational levels shot up, and standards of living began to grow and grow. Within a century, life expectancies had increased by two-thirds, average years of schooling had gone from single to double digits, and the productivity of workers and the pay they took home had doubled and doubled and then doubled again. With the United States leading the way, the rich world crossed a great divide—a divide separating centuries of slow growth, poor health, and anemic technical progress from one of hitherto undreamed-of material comfort and seemingly limitless economic potential. For the first time, rich countries experienced economic development that was both broad and deep, reaching all major segments of society and producing not just greater material comfort but also fundamental transformations in the health and life chances of those it touched.

The mixed economy lay at the heart of this success, in the United States no less than in other Western nations. Capitalism played an essential role, but it was not the new entrant on the economic stage; effective governance was. Public health measures made cities engines of innovation rather than incubators of illness. The meteoric expansion of public education increased not only individual opportunity but also the economic potential of entire societies. Investments in science, higher education, and defense spearheaded breakthroughs in medicine, transportation, and technology. Overarching rules and institutions tamed unstable financial markets and turned boombust cycles into more manageable ups and downs. Protections against excessive insecurity and abject destitution encouraged the forward-looking investments and social integration that sustained growth required. The mixed economy was a spectacularly positive- sum bargain: it redistributed power and resources, but as its impacts broadened, virtually everyone was made massively better off.

Government has unique capacities that allow it to solve problems that markets can't solve on their own.

In nations where the mixed economy took hold, the economy underwent spectacular growth. Not coincidentally, government did too. Indeed, it grew even more quickly. At the end of the nineteenth century, government spending (at all levels) accounted for around one in ten dollars of output in the wealthiest nations. By the end of the twentieth, it averaged over four in ten dollars, with the public sector accounting for six in ten dollars of GDP in the highest- spending rich nations. In some ways, these numbers overstate government's size, since much of government spending essentially shifts private income from one person or household to another rather than financing goods or services directly. Yet standard measures also understate the size of government, because they don't include many of the ways that government affects the economy: from regulation to protections against risk to the provision of legal safeguards. Suffice it to say that for all their imperfections and ambiguities, the numbers capture something real: government has grown much bigger.

Before looking at statistics such as these, one might assume that poor countries have large governments—at least compared with the size of their puny economies—and rich countries, small governments. After all, there are a couple of big tasks that governments have to do just to remain governments: provide at least a modicum of protection against internal violence and protect against external threats. These are pretty much fixed costs, or at least costs that vary with country and population size far more than economic heft, so one might expect that as the economy grows, the relative size of the state shrinks.

But that is not at all what happened. The richest countries expanded their governments the most. They upped their public spending dramatically during the period in which they grew most quickly, issued more regulations, expanded their legal systems, and offered implicit and explicit guarantees to private actors that were costless on paper but almost incalculably valuable in practice (such as serving as lenders of last resort). Modern growth occurred where, and only where, activist government emerged. And therein lies a big clue as to why the great divide was crossed.

Perhaps the most important thing that big states started doing was educating their citizens. Modern growth commenced when people rapidly increased their ability to do more with less. They were able to do more because they knew more, and they knew more, in part, because they were taught more. The beneficial forms of what the economist Robert Solow famously called "technical change"—the ideas and innovations that allow people to be more productive—rest on widespread public education that seeds scientific advances and equips workers with new skills. Indeed, economists have concluded that roughly a third of rising productivity is tied directly to increased education, with most of the rest due to general advances in knowledge.

Government was no less crucial to another pillar of modern prosperity, the physical infrastructure that helped make the scientific infrastructure possible and productive. Even before rich countries came to depend on public investments in science and technology for rapid growth, they depended on public investments in transportation and communications networks that linked together producers and their suppliers and consumers. Among other benefits, public infrastructure facilitated the rapid flow of materials and people across long distances, allowed manufacturers to benefit from economies of scale that supported modern assembly-line techniques, permitted innovations to diffuse and goods to reach far-flung consumers, and created opportunities for workers to find jobs that matched their skills.

THE LOGIC OF GOVERNMENT INTERVENTION

Why does it take a lot of government to get and keep prosperity? Because government has unique capacities—to enforce compliance, constrain or encourage action, and protect citizens from private predation—that allow it to solve problems that markets can't solve on their own. These problems are both economic and political; they concern areas in which markets tend to fall short and areas where market actors tend to distort democratic processes in pursuit of private advantage. And even beyond correcting market failures, government can play an important role in helping markets do better at serving human needs.

One important market failure comes in the underprovision of what economists call "public goods," valuable things that must be provided to everyone or no one. The classic example is a lighthouse. Its light is available to all ships navigating a coastline. There is no cost-effective way to limit the lighthouse's benefits to paying customers, so nobody has a reason to pay. And if no one pays, markets won't motivate anyone to provide the good. Public goods of this kind are prevalent in modern life. The biggest, most obvious example is national security, which consumes one-sixth of U.S. federal spending, but the same logic applies to infrastructure and fundamental scientific research, the latter of which is the cornerstone for technological innovation.

Another kind of market failure involves the effects of market operations on people who are neither buyers nor sellers. Economists call these effects "externalities," and a classic example of a negative externality is pollution. In an unregulated market, neither a factory owner nor a firm's customers have strong incentives to care about what happens to, say, the noxious byproducts of the factory's manufacturing processes. So in an unregulated market, the factory can spew toxins into the air or water with impunity. Where such externalities are present, the market prices for the goods in question will not reflect the true social costs (or, for positive externalities, the benefits) of the private transaction.

Externalities are always an issue, but they become a much bigger issue as economies develop. In dense, complex modern societies, externalities are ubiquitous, and the associated costs (or untapped benefits) of bad market signals, potentially momentous. They include the dangers to the financial system of excessive risk taking among bankers, the dangers to public health if children are not inoculated against disease or are exposed to brain-damaging levels of lead, and the forgone human potential (and squandered economic production) if children are not given a quality education. Even the spiral of underconsumption that follows a downturn can be seen as an externality: everyone retreating from consumer markets at once means more lost jobs and an economy that continues to underperform. What's individually rational is collectively destructive, and hence governments may need to step in to reverse the slide with countercyclical policies.

In complex societies, failures caused by incomplete or asymmetrically distributed information (when one party to a transaction knows a lot more than another) also become more ubiquitous. Insurance markets routinely fall short, for example, when buyers know more about the risks they face than do sellers (who then figure out many ways to exclude or limit coverage for those they fear will be costly). This is one reason why publicly provided or subsidized insurance has proved a mainstay of all rich countries, protecting people against risks they cannot protect themselves against and encouraging investments that entail such risk (such as investment in human capital that might lose value in a dynamic economy where needed skills change rapidly).

And it's not just that information can be incomplete or unevenly distributed. Although even broaching the subject invites charges of paternalism, the fact is that people can be very bad at making very important decisions when those decisions are complex, confusing, or involve long-term costs and benefits. As behavioral economics has increasingly shown, myopia and the difficulty of delaying gratification are important reasons for such negative outcomes as insufficient retirement savings and premature death due to smoking. In this context, government "nudges" or even more vigorous pushes—when informed by science and designed to preserve individual autonomy—can be enormously prosperity enhancing.

Because governments have chosen to intervene to provide public goods, counter negative externalities, and do some benign nudging, hundreds of millions of lives are now healthier, safer, and better protected against financial risk. In the United States and other rich democracies, the majority of government spending goes to social programs related to health care (Medicare and Medicaid) and retirement (Social Security), and the majority of regulation involves protection of the public from the operations of unscrupulous private actors. These programs are overwhelmingly popular even though they are also, as a rule, coercive. That is not a paradox; it's the point—because government is doing things that people need to get done but can't or won't do themselves.

FROM THE FOUNDERS TO THE PROGRESSIVES

The emergence of modern economies capable of generating unprecedented affluence has coincided with the emergence of activist government capable of extensive taxation, spending, regulation, and macroeconomic management. The United States' emergence as a world economic power in the latter half of the nineteenth century featured plenty of enterprising citizens seizing on the opportunities for economic advancement that the U.S. Constitution protected. But the role of the founders and their political heirs was much more direct. They built a state with the power to tax, spend, enforce, defend, and expand. Once in office, they often used the shrewd deployment of vast public lands as a substitute for taxation but with similar effects. They and their colleagues helped create a continental nation linked by infrastructure, governed by a federal legal system, and boasting the most educated work force in the world.

This trajectory was a reflection of the Constitution's purpose and design, not (as many charge today) a betrayal of them. The leading statesmen who gathered in Philadelphia in 1787 were keenly aware of the need for effective government authority. Indeed, they had become convinced that its absence was a mortal threat to the fledgling nation. Perhaps the most influential of them all, James Madison, put the point bluntly at the Virginia ratifying convention: "There never was a government without force. What is the meaning of government? An institution to make people do their duty. A government leaving it to a man to do his duty, or not, as he pleases, would be a new species of government, or rather no government at all." In designing a substitute for the loose Articles of Confederation, which had brought so much instability and vulnerability, the authors of the Constitution also put in place most of the basic instruments of governance that would become the seeds of the United States' economic flowering.

As the country reached its centenary, however, the sapling that had grown faced stiff new winds from concentrated corporate power. What came to be known as the Gilded Age is now sometimes portrayed as a glorious time of unchecked individual initiative to which the country should aspire to return. The lesson it actually teaches is very different: that a modern industrial economy cannot function without independent national authority. The business titans of the late nineteenth and early twentieth centuries were skillful in ways both laudable and despicable, but as the economist J. Bradford DeLong has argued, they were also just plain lucky. They came along when national markets were finally possible, they benefited from public land grants and loan guarantees, they capitalized on economies of scale that allowed early movers to bury rivals, and they then monetized future profits (likely or imagined) through volatile and manipulable financial markets.

The Progressives set out to rescue capitalism, not replace it.

The monopolistic capitalism that emerged during this era was unsustainable—economically, politically, and, although few paid attention to it at the time, ecologically. Prior government policies had been successful in promoting development. Without them, building the railroads likely would have taken decades longer, with a huge economic loss. But these policies fostered concentrated corporate power that the federal government lacked the capacity to govern effectively, and the costs to American society of that incapacity were skyrocketing. Workplace accidents soared as industrial and rail work expanded. The toxic financial assets of the era caused repeated economic crises. The social and environmental costs of industrialization were devastating. Weak and penetrated by private interests, courts provided little recourse, whether to victims of fraud, monopolies, accidents, or tainted food or medicine. And so long as government sat on the sidelines, the harms just kept multiplying. It was only a matter of time before a reaction set in, and eventually it did, in the form of the Progressive movement.

Theodore and Franklin Roosevelt, two of the movement's most prominent figures, were distant cousins and very different men. But they shared a conviction that government had to be strengthened to rebalance American democracy and ensure broadly distributed gains. Either could have said what Teddy declared in 1910: "The citizens of the United States must effectively control the mighty commercial forces which they have called into being."

Theodore Roosevelt would not live to see that goal achieved during his lifetime. The list of major reforms enacted in the first two decades of the twentieth century, under Roosevelt and Wilson, is long: the enfranchisement of women, the direct election of senators, the nation's first income tax, workers' compensation, the Clayton Antitrust Act, the establishment of the Federal Reserve, the first restrictions on money in politics, the first serious attempts at environmental preservation, and extensive new national regulations, including the Pure Food and Drug Act of 1906, which laid the foundation for the U.S. Food and Drug Administration. Yet Roosevelt died in 1919, on the eve of another decade of financial speculation and runaway inequality, during which public authority decayed while problems festered—until, of course, an economic crisis made continued inaction untenable once again.

Picking up where Theodore Roosevelt and Wilson had left off, Franklin Roosevelt put in place a broad range of policies that inserted government deeply into previously untouched areas of the U.S. political economy. The New Deal brought tougher financial oversight, including the creation of the Securities and Exchange Commission. With the National Labor Relations Act, it brought organized labor into the mixed economy's emerging system of countervailing power. With the Social Security Act, it introduced a widely popular system of social insurance that would protect the American middle class from some of the risks associated with modern capitalism. And with the emerging national system of taxes and spending, the New Deal added to the growing tool kit of macroeconomic management that would prevent or moderate future economic downturns.

Despite the interregnum of the 1920s, therefore, it makes sense to think of the two Roosevelts as bookending a long Progressive era. It was progressive because at crucial moments, nearly everyone in a position of high public leadership came to believe that the U.S. social contract needed updating. It was long because challenging entrenched elites proved difficult, and only persistent agitation and huge disruptions to the U.S. political order allowed the translation of these new beliefs into new governing arrangements.

THE HEYDAY OF THE MIXED ECONOMY

The Progressives set out to rescue capitalism, not replace it. The academic who oversaw the development of the Social Security Act, Edwin Witte, said of it, "Only to a very minor degree [did the act] modify the distribution of wealth, and it does not alter at all the fundamentals of our capitalistic and individualistic economy." The welfare state softened the sharp edges of capitalism without tight restrictions on economic dynamism. At the core of the new system that emerged was an exchange: the government would take much larger amounts of money from citizens than ever before, and then it would turn around and spend that money on various projects that benefited those same citizens, both individually and collectively.

Before the twentieth century, income taxes had barely existed in the United States, and before World War II, they had brought in no more than two percent of national income. By 1943, they raked in 11 percent, and the share of the population paying them skyrocketed from seven percent to 64 percent.

At first, most of the money went to the war effort, of course. But research in universities and industrial labs also benefited. And as scientists flocked to U.S. universities to join in the action, young Americans poured into college with funding from the GI Bill. Rivaling these investments in research and education, both in scale and in social return, were vast government outlays for highways, airports, waterways, and other forms of infrastructure. The interstate highway system began with Dwight Eisenhower's 1956 National Interstate and Defense Highways Act, which dedicated over $200 billion (in current dollars) to the cause and hiked the nationwide gas tax to provide highway financing.

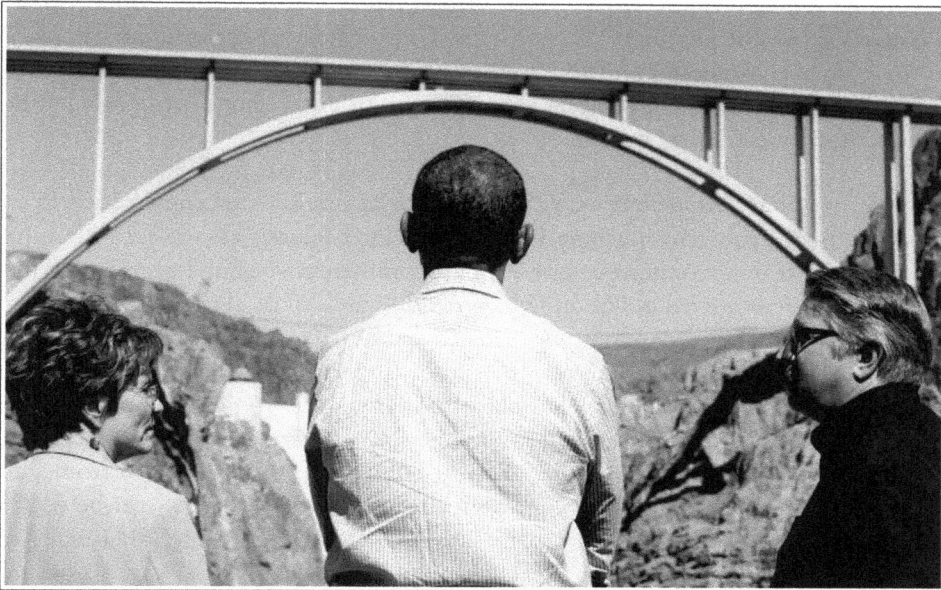

U.S. President Barack Obama visits the Hoover Dam in Boulder City, Nevada, October 2012.

New Deal programs devoted to economic security expanded as well. With Eisenhower's strong support, Congress extended Social Security to cover almost all Americans and made it generous enough to pull more of the elderly out of poverty, even as disability protections were added. National health insurance—proposed by President Harry Truman but opposed by the growing private health industry—never made it to the floor of Congress, but wartime wage and price controls that permitted supplemental benefits, the spread of collective bargaining, and tax breaks for health insurance helped push private coverage up to an eventual peak of around three-quarters of Americans by the mid-1970s. The federal government also subsidized and regulated private pensions that built on top of Social Security.

As these tax breaks suggest, the new U.S. state was no unchecked Leviathan. It commingled public and private spending, direct outlays and indirect subsidies, central direction and decentralized implementation. It fostered pluralistic competition for funds among researchers, contractors, and private intermediaries, as well as among states and localities. But it was enormously active and enormously successful—and soon its rewards would extend to groups that had yet to feel the warm sun of American prosperity.

In expanding rights for women and minorities—through statutes, judicial action, and the government's own example (most profoundly, in the armed services)—the nation was finding money on the table. Government policies also boosted the skills and opportunities of the least advantaged, where the returns on such investments were highest. As the federal government expanded, it did not merely extend opportunities to individuals on the periphery of prosperity. It also extended opportunities to places on the periphery, especially the South, injecting assistance and employment, housing and highways, development projects and defense jobs into regions previously left behind by modern economic growth.

As the postwar period wore on, U.S. leaders made another vital contribution to the country's rising prosperity, pushing to address market failures associated with an increasingly dense, interconnected, and complex commercial society. The most obvious breakthroughs concerned pollution, which rapidly came to be seen as a fundamental threat to quality of life requiring vigorous regulation. The federal government also improved protections for worker safety, and in response to the growing profile of activists such as Ralph Nader, it paid much more attention to vulnerable consumers in areas as diverse as tobacco and automobiles, using the power of the state to protect citizens from the predation of others and to limit the potential damage from their own myopic choices (such as smoking cigarettes or failing to wear a seat belt). The story of the United States' rise to richness is a story of an ongoing rebalancing of political institutions and economic realities, of public policies, social knowledge, and democratic demands. But the arc of that history bends toward a more extensive role for government, and for good reason: As the United States changed from an agricultural society into an industrial society and then a postindustrial society, the scale of economic activity and the interdependence and complexity of that activity grew, and so did the resulting damage. As the nation's leaders responded to these challenges and to pressures for action and inclusion from below, they came to recognize that making Americans healthier, better educated, and freer to pursue their own dreams—regardless of race, gender, and ethnicity, whatever the circumstances of their birth—made America richer, too.

THE BEGINNING OF THE BACKLASH

For roughly 30 years, from the early 1940s to the mid-1970s, the mixed economy of U.S. capitalism achieved unprecedented success, nurturing innovation, sustaining stability, and generating opportunity and prosperity. This successful model rested on a series of social and political understandings, compromises, and accommodations. Given their power in U.S. society, leading business figures were necessarily key participants in this success. Prominent Republicans became believers as well.

The most famous GOP convert was the general turned politician Eisenhower. He understood that the Republican Party needed to make its peace with most of the policy achievements of the previous two decades. In 1954, for example, Eisenhower privately ridiculed the desire of conservatives to roll back the New Deal: "Should any political party attempt to abolish social security, unemployment insurance, and eliminate labor laws and farm programs, you would not hear of that party again in our political history.

There is a tiny splinter group, of course, that believes you can do these things. … Their number is negligible and they are stupid." Eisenhower's point was that the mixed economy was an established reality and there was no going back.

Eisenhower's domestic policy agenda focused on economic growth, and Democrats would criticize him for his reluctance to rely on Keynesian policy to prime the economy. Yet his administration devoted substantial energy to policies designed to improve the country's long-term economic performance. And on economic issues, the moderate consensus continued after Eisenhower left office. Although John F. Kennedy famously adopted a more Keynesian stance on the budget (built around business-friendly tax cuts), in most respects his economic policies followed the tracks laid down in the 1950s. When the GOP veered right with Barry Goldwater's candidacy, and Lyndon Johnson tacked left with the inclusionary policies of the Civil Rights Act and the War on Poverty, much of the business establishment went with Johnson.

Richard Nixon was one of the last Republican leaders to embrace the mixed economy, and embrace it he did. Nixon's efforts to fashion a new majority involved positioning himself to the right of Democrats on issues of race and crime, but he was willing to be a moderate, even an activist, on matters related to the economy. He supported major extensions of the regulatory state, including big new initiatives for environmental and consumer protection. He favored a guaranteed annual income, a huge expansion of Social Security, and health-care reforms way to the left of what Bill Clinton or Barack Obama ever proposed.

Nixon's moderation was driven in part by political calculations. Encouraged by Daniel Patrick Moynihan, one of his leading advisers on domestic policy, he took the nineteenth-century British prime minister Benjamin Disraeli's "liberal Tory" stance as a model and sought to appeal to working-class and middle-class whites with his support for social insurance and his cautious backing of many of the new regulatory measures coming out of a Democratic Congress. But it wasn't all politics. Nixon accepted the notion that in a large and complex society, government had a fundamental role to play in fostering economic growth and social prosperity. This went beyond the macroeconomic management of boom-and-bust cycles and incorporated support for collective bargaining, extensive social insurance and a reasonable social safety net, the provision of crucial public goods, and interventions to tackle thorny market failures.

As the 1970s continued, however, the mixed economy came under concerted attack by a more powerful and more radical economic elite. At first, the economic and ideological components of this challenge were largely independent of each other. But over time they fused, as the increasing dominance of market-fundamentalist thinking on the right encouraged shifts in corporate behavior and public policy that exacerbated the intellectual and economic distinctiveness of the United States' new economic elite: the deregulation of finance, the slashing of top federal tax rates, growing links between the financial and the corporate sectors, an upward spiral of executive pay.

An industry of enablers sprang up, with journalists and think tanks and professional associations and lobbyists all helping push the new line, and eventually the movement captured its biggest prize, the Republican Party.

Ideas were crucial, especially in the initial right turn. Within conservative political and intellectual circles and in corporate boardrooms, elements of the fringe libertarian views of the novelist and philosopher Ayn Rand gained prominence. Randian thinking came in both soft and hard forms (an obsession with deficits, say, versus die-hard opposition to taxes and government spending), but in both forms, it had important implications for U.S. understandings of shared prosperity. The valorization of shareholders (even if it was often a cover for the acquisitive aims of top executives or investors planning hostile takeovers) challenged the notion that wealth was a social creation that rested on the efforts of multiple stakeholders, including labor and government. Instead, it implied that prosperity was generated solely by entrepreneurs and investors, thanks to their creativity and daring. In its radical manifestation, it even became something of a conspiracy theory, dividing the world into a persecuted minority that heroically generates prosperity and a freeloading majority that uses government to steal from this small, creative elite.

The conservative elite's turn against the mixed economy just kept going and going.

These ideas began to gain credence with the emergence of "stagflation," a stubborn combination of high inflation and economic stagnation that plagued the country in the second half of the 1970s and seemed to rebut the notion that government could manage the economy effectively. But what occurred was not simply an ideological shift; opposition to the mixed economy took off because it intersected with and guided powerful economic interests that were themselves gaining political influence. Facing meager profits and depressed stock prices, business leaders mobilized to lobby Washington as never before. They accepted the diagnosis offered by the new market fundamentalists that the source of their woes was not foreign competition or deindustrialization or hostile financial players but rather unions and government intervention in the economy.

Once the door opened to the new antigovernment stance, policy and profit seeking reinforced each other. The free- market movement advocated financial deregulation and tax cuts, and these policies helped fuel a rapid and sweeping shift in corporate America. Companies faced intense pressure to become better integrated into an expanding global economy. Even more important, they faced intense pressure to become better integrated into an expanding financial sector. As corporate America orbited ever closer to Wall Street, it adopted Wall Street's priorities as its own: immediate stock returns, corporate financial engineering, and extremely high executive pay closely tied to share prices. Meanwhile, the constraint on top management created by organized labor was rapidly weakening, as unions struggled in an increasingly hostile climate.

The result was not just enormous fortunes going to a narrower and narrower slice of executives. It was also an enormous shift in power toward a new corporate elite that was much more hostile to the mixed economy, much less constrained by moderates in government or by organized labor, and much more in tune with the new celebration of the market.

In retrospect, the economic tumult of the 1970s looks less baffling than it did at the time. The surge of inflation reflected both singular shocks (notably, the 1973–74 OPEC oil embargo) and obvious policy mistakes (Johnson's guns-and- butter spending and Nixon's urging of loose monetary policy to secure his reelection). Productivity growth slowed as the burst of economic activity after World War II gave way to the more normal expansion of rich countries at the edge of the technological frontier. And the United States faced greater competition from its affluent trading partners as they recovered from wartime devastation.

But inflation captured the public's attention and drove the increasingly panicked national debate, eventually leading Jimmy Carter to appoint the prominent inflation hawk Paul Volcker to head the Federal Reserve. As expected, he raised interest rates sharply, triggering the worst economic downturn since the 1930s. Not only did the recession probably cost Carter the 1980 election; it battered the economic reputation of the Democratic Party. The episode paved the way for Ronald Reagan to pursue a very different vision of government's relationship to the economy.

But however sobering the economic challenges of the 1970s might have been, they did not need to tarnish the entire edifice of the mixed economy. Getting macroeconomic policy on a sounder track and confronting heightened foreign competition did not require unwinding government's constructive role in ensuring broad prosperity. The social institution of the mixed economy could have been updated; the balance between effective public authority and dynamic private markets could have been recalibrated rather than rejected. Nor did popular pressures demand radical change. Voters may have turned right as inflation increased, but the conservative shift in public opinion was short lived. It was the conservative elite's turn against the mixed economy that just kept going and going, even intensifying over time, and it was that which ended up bankrolling and driving the ideological warfare that ensued.

BACK TO THE FUTURE

When Eisenhower delivered his first State of the Union address, he drew on a broad reservoir of support for the mixed economy. He took for granted that government made fundamental contributions to shared prosperity. Those within his party who thought otherwise were marginalized. Business leaders, too, recognized that they had to engage with government and labor as partners. Many genuinely accepted the partnership, but all understood that they had to accommodate it.

Forty years later, when Clinton took the podium to deliver his inaugural address, the world looked different. The reservoir of enthusiasm for government was dry, baked away by the relentless attacks on government that politicians of both parties had found were the surest way to gain national office. Declining public trust eroded support for active government and created a political vacuum that powerful private interests filled. A revitalized Republican Party led the assault. Yet even the party of government—and those, such as Clinton, who led it—found the spiral of anti-Washington sentiment hard to escape, especially as those powerful private interests became increasingly central sources of financial support.

The corporate world had changed as well. The financial restructuring that had begun in the 1980s had reshaped the character, leadership, and culture of American business. Among those favored by these changes, older understandings of what produced prosperity had given way to new conceptions of the relationship between business and government, the process of wealth creation, and the contribution of managers versus workers—conceptions sharply at odds with those supporting the mixed economy. In the new corporate world, business leaders who praised the active role of government or were willing to engage with political leaders to pursue broad prosperity were harder to find.

In this new climate, the excesses and inadequacies of government loomed larger than its benefits. Some of this frustration was, and continues to be, entirely legitimate. American government has indeed become less effective. The lawmaking process has become dysfunctional. Public policy is more beholden to narrow and deep-pocketed interests. Political attacks and pervasive public distrust make government less capable, which in turn provides fodder for more attacks and greater distrust. That this vicious cycle has been pushed along by smear attacks and sabotage campaigns does not make it any less real.

But just because government often performs tasks less well than it could or should doesn't mean that we would be better off without it, or even with less of it. The net benefits of modern government are enormous—at the level of major programs and, even more clearly, at the level of governance as a whole.

The mixed economy remains a spectacular achievement. Over the past century, the United States and other advanced democratic countries leapt across the Great Divide. They broke from the entirety of prior human existence, in which life was nasty, brutish, and short for almost everyone, and entered an era in which most citizens could look forward to long lives, a real education, and previously unimaginable material comfort. By combining the power of markets with a strong dose of public authority, they achieved unprecedented affluence.

The good news, moreover, is that these positive-sum achievements don't have to stop coming. Despite today's pessimism, many opportunities to make society better off still beckon, in part because for decades Washington has not been using government to best effect. But the bad news is that for this to happen, the nation's ideological and political climate must begin to shift, and the great American amnesia must finally lift.

Many changes have swept the U.S. economy since the 1970s. Yet the country's biggest problem is not a lack of attractive policy options. The United States' biggest problem is its politics. Roads, bridges, and transportation networks can be rebuilt, scientific research can flourish, and educational funding can be provided from early childhood through college—if only there were a renewed commitment to using activist government on behalf of the public good. The growth of health-care spending could be slowed, pollution could be diminished further, renewable energy could be sped toward feasibility. It is possible for Americans to live in a society that is not just fairer and more contented but richer as well. There may not be a free lunch, but there are lots of cheap, delicious, and highly nutritional lunches just waiting to be eaten, simply by returning to the mixed-economy playbook of a couple of generations ago, with appropriate updating for what has been learned since then.

In many specific areas, of course, Americans still believe that the public sector has a vital role. They support government regulation of the environment and government funding of education. They strongly endorse Social Security, Medicare, and most other social programs. They believe that political leaders have a responsibility to manage the economy. What has changed is that voters have become profoundly skeptical that government has the capacity or inclination to foster broad prosperity, especially when doing so requires it to take on new or newly intensified challenges or confront powerful entrenched interests. To build a mixed economy for the twenty-first century, a critical mass of citizens—and their leaders—has to believe once again that government can address their most pressing concerns.

The framing of "government versus the market" has become so ubiquitous in modern culture that most Americans now take it for granted. The hostility of the right is unceasing and mostly unanswered. Eloquent leaders often defend individual programs but too rarely defend the vital need for effective governance. Politicians facing electoral pressures participate in a spiral of silence. Chastened by government's low standing, they reinforce rather than try to reverse it.

Rhetoric is only one part of the problem. Cowed policymakers also design programs that send much the same message. The political scientist Suzanne Mettler has documented the increasing tendency to "submerge" policies so that the role of government is hidden from those who receive benefits. These subterranean policies include tax breaks for private savings for education and retirement and a reliance on private companies and contractors even when these proxies are less efficient than public provision. These submerged benefits are usually bad policies. More important, they are even worse politics. Voters who don't recognize government in action are not likely to appreciate what government does. Nor are they likely to form an accurate picture of government's role, seeing only its visible redistribution and not the vast number of ways in which it enables prosperity.

To get to that more realistic starting point will require a serious and prolonged investment in ideas. The crisis of public authority is a consequence of orchestrated, persistent efforts to tear down government and a long spiral of silence in response. To shake free of the amnesia about the benefits of a mixed economy and rebalance the national conversation will take many years of leadership and activism. The intellectual and organizational foundations of effective public authority will have to be rebuilt. Reform must be a multifront, interdependent effort in which robust but realistic steps steadily build trust and momentum toward a revitalized mixed economy.

The specific arrangements that enabled the U.S. economic model of the last century are dead and buried. But it is possible to build a new model for economic success, on new political foundations, to deepen prosperity in the twenty-first century. And today's complex and interdependent knowledge economy offers tremendous opportunities for positive-sum bargains that will strengthen both U.S. capitalism and the health of U.S. society. Grasping these opportunities, however, requires a mixed economy—the strong thumb of government as well as the nimble fingers of the market. This is the truth that both history and economic theory confirm: the government that governs best needs to govern quite a bit.

JACOBS. HACKER is Director of the Institution for Social and Policy Studies and Stanley B. Resor Professor of Political Science at Yale University. PAUL PIERSON is John Gross Professor of Political Science at the University of California at Berkeley. They are the authors of *American Amnesia: How the War on Government Led Us to Forget What Made America Prosper* (Simon & Schuster, 2016), from which this essay is adapted. Copyright © 2016 by JacobS. Hacker and Paul Pierson. Printed by permission.

The End of the Old Israel

How Netanyahu Has Transformed the Nation

Aluf Benn

People wave flags at a convoy transporting the body of an Israeli woman killed in the recent violence between Israelis and Palestinians, near Efrat, a Jewish settlement in the West Bank, January 2016.

Israel—at least the largely secular and progressive version of Israel that once captured the world's imagination—is over. Although that Israel was always in some ways a fantasy, the myth was at least grounded in reality. Today that reality has changed, and the country that has replaced it is profoundly different from the one its founders imagined almost 70 years ago. Since the last elections, in March 2015, a number of slow-moving trends have accelerated dramatically. Should they continue, they could soon render the country unrecognizable.

Already, the transformation has been dramatic. Israel's current leaders—headed by Prime Minister Benjamin Netanyahu, who metamorphosed after the election from a risk-averse conservative into a right-wing radical—see democracy as synonymous with unchecked majority rule and have no patience for restraints such as judicial review or the protection of minorities. In their view, Israel is a Jewish state and a democratic state—in that order. Only Jews should enjoy full rights, while gentiles should be treated with suspicion. Extreme as it sounds, this belief is now widely held: a Pew public opinion survey published in March found that 79 percent of Jewish Israelis supported "preferential treatment" for Jews—a thinly veiled euphemism for discrimination against non-Jews.

Meanwhile, the two-state solution to the conflict with the Palestinians has been taken off the table, and Israel is steadily making its occupation of East Jerusalem and the West Bank permanent. Human rights groups and dissidents who dare criticize the occupation and expose its abuses are denounced by officials, and the government has sought to pass new laws restricting their activities. Arab-Jewish relations within the country have hit a low point, and Israel's society is breaking down into its constituent tribes.

Netanyahu thrives on such tribalism, which serves his lifelong goal of replacing Israel's traditional elite with one more in tune with his philosophy. The origins of all these changes predate the current prime minister, however. To truly under- stand them, one must look much further back in Israel's history: to the country's founding, in 1948.

THE OLD MAN AND THE NEW JEW

Modern Israel was created by a group of secular socialists led by David Ben-Gurion, who would become the state's first prime minister. "The Old Man," as he was known, sought to create a homeland for a new type of Jew: a warrior-pioneer who would plow the land with a gun on his back and then read poetry around a bonfire when the battle was won. (This "new Jew" was mythologized, most memorably, by Paul Newman in the film Exodus.) Although a civilian, Ben-Gurion was a martial leader. He oversaw the fledgling state's victory in its War of Independence against Israel's Arab neighbors and the Palestinians, most of whom were then exiled. And when the war was over, the Old Man oversaw the creation of the Israel Defense Forces (IDF), which he designed to serve as (among other things) the new country's main tool for turning its polyglot Jewish immigrants into Hebrew-speaking citizens.

Ben-Gurion was a leftist but not a liberal. Following independence, he put Israel's remaining Arab residents under martial law (a condition that lasted until 1966) and expropriated much of their land, which he gave to Jewish communities. His party, Mapai (the forerunner of Labor), controlled the economy and the distribution of jobs. Ben-Gurion and his cohort were almost all Ashkenazi (of eastern European origin), and they discriminated against the Sephardic Jews (known in Israel as the Mizrahim), who came from Arab states such as Iraq, Morocco, Tunisia, and Yemen. Ben-Gurion also failed to appreciate the power of religion, which he believed would wither away when confronted with secular modernity. He therefore allowed the Orthodox to preserve their educational autonomy under the new state—thereby ensuring and underwriting the creation of future generations of religious voters.

In recent years, as the Israeli public has shifted rightward, so has Netanyahu—which has allowed him to more openly indulge his true passions.

For all Ben-Gurion's flaws, his achievements were enormous and should not be underestimated: he created one of the most developed states in the postcolonial world, with a world-class military, including a nuclear deterrent, and top scientific and technological institutions. His reliance on the IDF as a melting pot also worked well, effectively assimilating great numbers of new Israelis. This reliance on the military—along with its battlefield victories in 1948, 1956, and 1967—helped cement the centrality of the IDF in Israeli society. To this day, serving in the military's more prestigious units is the surest way to get ahead in the country. The army has supplied many of the nation's top leaders, from Yitzhak Rabin and Ezer Weizman to Ehud Barak and Ariel Sharon, and every chief of staff or intelligence head instantly becomes an unofficial candidate for high office on retirement.

The first major challenge to Ben-Gurion's idea of Israel arrived on Yom Kippur in 1973, when Egypt and Syria launched a surprise attack that managed to catch the IDF unawares. Although Israel ultimately won the war, it suffered heavy losses, and the massive intelligence failure traumatized the nation. Like the United Kingdom after World War I, Israel emerged technically victorious but shorn of its sense of invincibility.

Less than four years later, Menachem Begin—the founder of Israel's right wing—capitalized on this unhappiness and on Sephardic grievances to hand Labor its first-ever defeat at the polls. Taking power at the head of a new coalition called Likud (Unity), Begin forged an alliance with Israel's religious parties, which felt more at home with a Sabbath-observing conservative. To sweeten the deal, his government accelerated the building of Jewish settlements in the West Bank (which appealed to religious Zionists) and offered numerous concessions to the ultra-Orthodox, such as generous educational subsidies.

Begin was a conservative and nationalist. But the decades he'd spent in the opposition had taught him to respect dissent and debate. As prime minister, therefore, he always defended judicial independence, and he refrained from purging Labor loyalists from the top echelons of the civil service and the IDF. As a consequence, his revolution, important though it was, was only a partial one. Under Begin's leadership, Israel's old left-wing elite lost its cabinet seats. But it preserved much of its influence, holding on to top positions in powerful institutions such as the media and academia. And the

Supreme Court remained stocked with justices who, while officially nonpartisan, nevertheless represented a liberal worldview of human and civil rights.

BIBI'S BAPTISM

Although Likud has governed Israel for most of the years since then, the left's ongoing control over many other facets of life has given rise to a deep sense of resentment on the right. No one has felt that grievance more keenly than Netanyahu, who long dreamed of finishing Begin's incomplete revolution. "Bibi," as Netanyahu is known, first won the premiership in 1996, but it would take him decades to accomplish his goal.

Netanyahu's initial election came shortly after the assassination of Rabin. The years prior to Rabin's death had been dominated by the Oslo peace process between Israel and the Palestine Liberation Organization (PLO), and that same peace process would become the focus of his successor's first term as well.

Netanyahu opposed Oslo from the very beginning. Then as now, he saw Israel as a Jewish community besieged by hostile Arabs and Muslims who wanted to destroy it. He considered the Arab-Israeli conflict a perpetual fact of life that could be managed but would never be resolved. The West—which, in his view, was anti-Semitic, indifferent, or both—couldn't be counted on to help, and so Israel's leaders were duty bound to prevent a second Holocaust through a combination of smart diplomacy and military prowess. And they couldn't afford to worry about what the rest of the world thought of them. Indeed, one of Netanyahu's main domestic selling points has always been his willingness to stand up to established powers, whether they take the form of the U.S. president or the UN General Assembly (where Netanyahu served as Israel's representative from 1984 to 1988 and first caught his nation's attention). Netanyahu loves lecturing gentiles in his perfect English, and much of the Israeli public loves these performances. He may go overboard at times—as when, last October, he suggested that Adolf Hitler had gotten the idea to kill Europe's Jews from Amin al-Husseini, the grand mufti of Jerusalem during World War II. Historians of all stripes scoffed at the claim, but many ordinary Israelis were indifferent to its inaccuracy.

During his first term, Netanyahu connected his domestic and international agendas by blaming the leftism of Israel's old elite for the country's foreign policy mistakes. To prevent more missteps in the future, he borrowed a page from the U.S. conservative playbook and vowed to fight the groupthink at Israel's universities and on its editorial boards—a way of thinking that, he argued, had led the country to Oslo. In a 1996 interview with the Haaretz columnist Ari Shavit, Netanyahu complained about his delegitimization "by the nomenklatura of the old regime," adding that "the problem is that the intellectual structure of Israeli society is unbalanced." He pledged to create new, more conservative institutions to rewrite the national narrative.

But Netanyahu's political inexperience worked against him. His tenure was rocked by controversy, from his reckless provocations of the Palestinians and of Jordan to a scandal caused by his wife's mistreatment of household employees.

Israel's old elites closed ranks, and, with the support of the Clinton administration, they forced Netanyahu into another deal with the Palestinian leader Yasir Arafat. The 1998 Wye River memorandum—the last formal agreement that Israel and the Palestinians have signed to this day—triggered early elections in May 1999, after several small, hard-right parties abandoned Netanyahu's coalition in protest. Barak and the Labor Party emerged victorious.

Both Barak, a decorated former head of the IDF, and Sharon, who replaced Netanyahu at the helm of Likud and became prime minister himself in 2001, represented a return to the Ben-Gurion model of farmer turned soldier turned statesman. Their ascent thus restored the old order—at least temporarily—and made Netanyahu seem like a historical fluke.

Israeli Prime Minister Benjamin Netanyahu at a weekly cabinet meeting in the Golan Heights, April 2016.

A MODERATE MASK

But Netanyahu saw things differently, and he spent the next decade plotting his return to power. Following Sharon's reelection in 2003, Netanyahu become finance minister, although he resigned on the eve of the August 2005 unilateral pullout from Gaza. When Sharon created a new centrist party, Kadima (Forward), shortly after the withdrawal, Netanyahu took over the remnants of Likud. But he lost the next election, in March 2006, to Ehud Olmert, who had replaced the ailing Sharon as head of Kadima.

Olmert had pledged to follow through on his mentor's vision by withdrawing Israel from most of the West Bank. But in July, his plans were disrupted when he let Hezbollah draw him into a pointless and badly managed war in Lebanon. His subsequent effort to negotiate a comprehensive peace deal with the Palestinians, launched in Annapolis, Maryland, in late 2007, led nowhere. Meanwhile, Netanyahu's credibility and popularity were boosted that same year when Hamas, well armed with rockets, seized control of Gaza—just as he'd predicted. So when Olmert announced his resignation over corruption charges in the summer of 2008 (he ultimately went to jail earlier this year on different charges), Netanyahu was ready to pounce.

His revival was further aided by the sudden appearance in 2007 of what would become the most important of what Netanyahu called independent sources of thought. Israel Hayom (Israel Today) is a free daily newspaper owned by the American casino magnate Sheldon Adelson, and ever since its launch, it has provided Netanyahu with a loud and supportive media megaphone. By 2010, Israel Hayom had become the country's most-read weekday newspaper, printing 275,000 copies a day. And its front page has consistently read like Bibi's daily message: lauding his favorites, denouncing his rivals, boasting about Israel's achievements, and downplaying negative news.

With Olmert out of the picture, Netanyahu returned to office on March 31, 2009. Eager to prove that he was no longer the scandal-plagued firebrand who'd been voted out of office a decade before, however, and fearing pressure from the new U.S. president, Barack Obama, he once again was forced to shelve his long-term plans for elite replacement. Instead of undermining his enemies, he shifted to the center, recruiting several retired Likud liberals to vouch for the "new Bibi" and join his cabinet, and forging a coalition with Labor under Barak, who stayed on as defense minister (a job he'd held under Olmert). Together, Netanyahu and Barak spent much of the next four years working on an ultimately unrealized plan to bomb Iran's nuclear facilities.

In June 2009, ten days after Obama's Cairo address, Netanyahu sought to reinforce his new centrist credentials by endorsing the idea of Palestinian statehood in a speech. True to form, however, the prime minister imposed a condition: the Palestinians would first have to recognize Israel as a Jewish state. Mahmoud Abbas, the Palestinian president, instantly rejected the idea. But the move enhanced Netanyahu's moderate credentials anyway.

And it helped get Obama off his back—but not before the U.S. president convinced Netanyahu to accept a ten-month freeze on new residential construction in the West Bank settlements. The freeze was meaningless, however, since it didn't change the facts on the ground or facilitate serious peace talks. And soon after it expired, Republicans won control of the House of Representatives in the U.S. midterm election, creating a firewall against any further pressure from Washington. Obama soon lost interest in the thankless peace process. Although his rocky relationship with Netanyahu led to many juicy newspaper and magazine stories, it had little effect on Israel's internal politics, since most Israelis also distrusted the U.S. president, and still do; a global poll released in December 2015 found that Obama had a lower favorability rating in Israel than almost anywhere else, with only Russians, Palestinians, and Pakistanis expressing greater disapproval.

Any remaining pressure on Netanyahu to pursue peace with the Palestinians evaporated soon after the Arab Spring erupted. Hosni Mubarak's regime in Egypt collapsed, threatening a cornerstone of Israel's security strategy; Syria sank into a bloody civil war; and a terrifying new nemesis, the Islamic State (also known as ISIS), appeared on the scene. These events unexpectedly bolstered Israel's position in several ways: Russia and the United States ultimately joined forces to eliminate most of Syria's chemical weapons, and the conservative governments of Jordan, Saudi Arabia, the United Arab Emirates, and (after the 2013 counterrevolution) Egypt strengthened their ties with Jerusalem (albeit unofficially in most cases). But the regional carnage and turmoil horrified Israeli voters, who told themselves: if this is what the Arabs are capable of doing to one another, imagine what they would do to us if we gave them the chance.

Nonetheless, peace and security played an uncharacteristically minor role in the next election, in January 2013. Instead, the race was dominated by social issues, including the rapidly rising costs of housing and food staples in Israel. Such concerns helped usher in a new class of freshman politicians, who replaced old-timers such as Barak. But none of them was able to overcome the incumbent's experience and savvy, and after reengaging with his right- wing base and merging with another conservative party led by former Foreign Minister Avigdor Lieberman, Netanyahu won the election.

In the summer of 2014, following one last push for peace with Abbas (this time led by U.S. Secretary of State John Kerry), war broke out between Israel and Hamas. The discovery of dozens of tunnels dug by Hamas into Egyptian and Israeli territory put another big scare into the Israeli public and prompted a prolonged ground operation—the bloodiest conflict of the Netanyahu era. During 50 days of fighting, more than 2,000 Palestinians and 72 Israelis, mostly soldiers, were killed. Israel's Jewish population overwhelmingly supported the war, but the fighting caused communal tensions in the country to explode. Thousands of Arab Israelis—who identified with the suffering in Gaza and were tired of their own abuse by the police and their increasing marginalization under Netanyahu—protested against the war. Hundreds were arrested, and other Arabs employed in the public sector were reportedly threatened with firing after criticizing the conflict on Facebook.

Israel has already become far less tolerant and open to debate than it used to be.

THE NEW RIGHT

Around the same time, personal animosities within Netanyahu's coalition started to pull it apart. Netanyahu was unable to prevent Israel's parliament, the Knesset, from electing Reuven Rivlin, a longtime Likud rival, to the largely symbolic presidency. And several of the prime minister's erstwhile allies, including Lieberman, endorsed a bill that would have forced Israel Hayom to start charging its readers. (The bill never made it past a preliminary hearing.) In December, the government finally collapsed, and the Knesset called an early election.

Likud went into the 2015 race trailing in the polls. The public was angry with Netanyahu over a small-time financial scandal involving his wife and over the stalemated result of the war with Hamas. The Zionist Union, a new centrist coalition led by Labor's Isaac Herzog, seemed poised to form the next government. But the uncharismatic Labor leader proved no match for his wilier, more experienced adversary. Netanyahu tacked right—scoring an unprecedented invitation to address the U.S. Congress (which he used to denounce the nuclear deal the Obama administration was negotiating with Iran) and stealing votes from smaller conservative parties by promising not to allow a Palestinian state to be established on his watch. Then, on election day, he released a video in which he claimed that "Arab voters are heading to the polling stations in droves. Left-wing NGOs are bringing them in buses." The statement wasn't true, but it effectively tapped into Jewish voters' anxiety and racism and won Likud the election: Likud emerged with 30 seats; the Zionist Union earned 24.

In Israel's fractious parliamentary system, votes alone don't determine who takes power, however; that gets decided during the coalition-building process that inevitably follows each election. In this case, the electoral math left Netanyahu, who was 31 seats short of a majority, with two choices: he could form a national unity coalition with Herzog and the ultra-Orthodox, or he could forge a narrow but ideologically cohesive alliance with several smaller center- and far-right parties.

Choosing Herzog would have created a wider coalition and allowed Netanyahu to show a more moderate face to the world. But the prime minister, who was sick of acting like a centrist, picked the latter course instead. That left him with a very narrow, one-seat majority in the Knesset. But it also gave him his first undiluted hard-right government since his 2009 comeback—one that would finally allow him to realize his long-deferred dream of remaking Israel's establishment.

Although Netanyahu is both secular and Ashkenazi, his new allies are mostly Mizrahim—long ostracized from Israel's centers of power, even though they represent a large segment of the Jewish population—and religious Zionists, who are known for their knitted yarmulkes, are fiercely committed to (and often live in) West Bank settlements, and have, in recent years, come to hold many prominent positions in the army, the security services, and the civil service.

These groups are most vocally represented by three members of the current government: Likud's Miri Regev, the minister of culture; Naftali Bennett, the minister of education and head of Habayit Hayehudi (Jewish Home), a religious Zionist party that he built out of the ashes of the old National Religious Party; and Ayelet Shaked, Bennett's longtime sidekick and now the minister of justice. Regev is Sephardic—her family came to Israel from Morocco—and a former brigadier general in the IDF, where she served as chief spokesperson during the Gaza pullout. Bennett, the son of American immigrants, served in the Israeli special forces and then made a fortune as a high-tech entrepreneur. He is both a model product of the "start-up nation" and the epitome of the religious, fiercely nationalist, pro-settlement leader (although he himself lives comfortably within the Green Line). Shaked, meanwhile, was a computer engineer before joining politics; despite her membership in the Jewish Home, she is neither religious nor a settler. Both she and Bennett worked directly for Netanyahu in Likud a decade ago, when he was the opposition leader, but they broke with him over personal quarrels in 2008.

AMIR COHEN / REUTERS

Changing of the guard: Netanyahu at a memorial service for Ben-Gurion, November 2014.

Like the prime minister, Regev, Bennett, and Shaked are skilled, media-savvy communicators. In keeping with Israeli tradition, all three have complicated, "frenemy" relationships with Netanyahu. Regev climbed the ranks of Likud without the prime minister's sponsorship, and Netanyahu has never forgiven Bennett and Shaked for their betrayals; the two are never invited to join him at his residence or on his plane. Yet so far, they have not let their personal grievances block the pursuit of their shared interests. Netanyahu needs Bennett and Shaked to keep his coalition afloat, and he needs Regev to maintain his support among Sephardic Israelis, an important Likud constituency. And there are no real ideological differences among the four politicians. Netanyahu is thus happy to let the others lead the charge against the old guard—and to take the heat for it as well.

Since taking office last year, the three ministers have readily obliged him. Regev—who likes to rail against what she calls "the haughty left-wing Ashkenazi elite" and once proudly told an interviewer that she'd never read Chekhov and didn't like classical music—has sought to give greater prominence to Sephardic culture and to deprive "less than patriotic" artists of government subsidies. Bennett's ministry has rewritten public school curricula to emphasize the country's Jewish character; it recently introduced a new high school civics textbook that depicts Israel's military history through a religious Zionist lens and sidelines the role of its Arab minority. In December 2015, Bennett even banned Borderlife, a novel describing a romance between a young Jewish Israeli woman and a Palestinian man, from high school reading lists.

Shaked, for her part, has vowed to reduce judicial interference in the work of the executive and the Knesset by appointing more conservative justices to the Supreme Court next year, when four to five seats (out of 15) will open up. She has also made good use of her position as head of the cabinet committee on legislation, which decides which bills the executive will support in the Knesset. The committee has recently promoted several draft laws designed to curb political expression. One, aimed at non-Zionist Arab legislators, would allow the Knesset to suspend a member indefinitely for supporting terrorism, rejecting Israel's status as a Jewish state, or inciting racism. Another, which Shaked has personally championed, would shame human rights groups by publicly identifying those that get more than half their funding from foreign governments. (So far, none of these bills, or even more restrictive measures put forward by Likud backbenchers—such as one that would label left-wing nongovernmental organizations "foreign agents" and another that would triple the jail sentence for flag burning—has been passed.)

Meanwhile, Netanyahu is doing his part as well. After last year's election, he insisted on holding on to the communications portfolio himself, giving him the last word on any media-related legislation. This move has given him unprecedented leverage over Israel's television and telecommunications networks, which have grown leery of doing anything to alienate the prime minister.

Many of the government's recent actions, such as Regev's promotion of Sephardic culture, seem designed to address the traditional disenfranchisement of Israel's Mizrahim and citizens living in the country's "periphery" (that is, far from the central Tel Aviv–Jerusalem corridor). Other measures are aimed at promoting social mobility. Yet virtually all of them have had a clear political goal as well: to reduce, if not eliminate, the domestic opposition to Israel's occupation of the West Bank, which Netanyahu and his allies want to make permanent. By portraying the shrinking peace camp and its supporters as unpatriotic stooges of foreign anti-Semites, the government hopes to delegitimize them and build a consensus around its hard-right policies.

The strategy seems to be working. One example: in a poll conducted last December of Israeli Jews, 53 percent of those surveyed supported outlawing Breaking the Silence, a veterans' group that aims to expose the harsh realities of the occupation by publishing wrenching testimonials of soldiers who have served in the West Bank.

DAGGERS DRAWN

Late last summer, after years of relative quiet, violence erupted in the West Bank and inside Israel. The first intifada (1987–93) was characterized by mass protests and stone throwing; during the second intifada (2000–2005), organized Palestinian suicide bombings and large-scale military reprisals by Israel caused thousands of casualties. This time, the so-called loners' intifada has taken a more privatized form. Acting on their own, young Palestinian men and women have used knives and homemade guns to attack Israeli military and police checkpoints or civilians at flash points such as the settlements and Jerusalem's Old City. So far, 34 Israelis have died in these assaults. Almost all the perpetrators have been arrested or shot on the spot—to date, about 200 Palestinians have been killed—but more have kept coming.

The loners' intifada has presented the current government with its toughest test so far. Netanyahu has always claimed to be tough on terror and has portrayed his opponents as softies. Yet he and his top aides have seemed clueless in the face of the rising violence. Instead of stanching the bloodshed, they have redoubled their attacks on those they deem enemies within: human rights groups and Arab Israeli politicians. And the center-left parties, worried about looking unpatriotic, have gone along with him. In April, Herzog urged Labor to "stop giving the impression that we are always Arab-lovers." And Yair Lapid, the head of the opposition Yesh Atid (There's a Future) party—another centrist faction—has called on the army and the police to ease their rules of engagement and "shoot to kill whoever takes out a knife or a screwdriver or whatever." Highlighting the danger of such rhetoric, in late March, B'Tselem, a respected human rights group, released a video taken in Hebron showing an Israeli soldier executing a Palestinian suspect who had already been shot and was lying, bleeding, on the street.

Instead of remorse, the Hebron shooting unleashed a wave of ugly nationalism among many Israeli Jews. The military high command quickly detained the soldier and declared his action immoral, unlawful, and undisciplined. Yet in a public opinion poll conducted several days after the incident, 68 percent of respondents supported the shooting, and 57 percent said that the soldier should not face criminal prosecution. Far-right politicians, including Bennett, defended the killer, and Netanyahu, who had initially supported the military brass, quickly closed ranks with his right-wing rivals and called the shooter's parents to express his support. When Moshe Yaalon, the defense minister, nonetheless insisted on a criminal investigation, he was roundly attacked on social media for his stand. After Netanyahu seemed to side with Yaalon's critics, their quarrel escalated, and in May, Yaalon resigned. Announcing his decision, Yaalon remarked, "I fought with all my might against manifestations of extremism, violence, and racism in Israeli society, which are threatening its sturdiness and also trickling into the IDF, hurting it."

Netanyahu's government will keep trying to cement as many changes as possible to Israeli society and the Israeli establishment.

That Yaalon of all people could be subjected to such treatment shows just how much Israel has changed in recent years. A Likud leader and former IDF chief of staff, Yaalon is no leftist: he supported Oslo but later changed his mind when, as the head of military intelligence, he witnessed Arafat's duplicity firsthand. Yet Yaalon believes in the importance of a secular state and the rule of law. That marked him as one of the last of the Ben-Gurion-style old guard still in office. And those credentials were enough to incite the online mob. It didn't matter that he had an impressive military record, opposed the peace process, or supported settlement expansion. In Netanyahu's Israel, merely insisting on due process for a well-documented crime is now enough to win you the enmity of the new elite and its backers.

THE PERMANENT PRIME MINISTER

One of the ways Netanyahu has retained power for so long—he's now Israel's second-longest-serving leader, after Ben-Gurion—has been by tailoring his politics to match public opinion. In 2009, he leaned toward the center because he feared Obama and wanted to dispel his own reputation for recklessness. In recent years, as the Israeli public has shifted rightward, so has he—which has allowed him to more openly indulge his true passions.

Throughout this period, Netanyahu has benefited from one other key asset: the lack of any serious challenger, either inside or outside Likud. Since returning to power in 2009, he has consistently beaten all other plausible candidates for prime minister in public opinion polls—by large margins. Within Likud, Netanyahu has managed to sideline a series of aspirants, such as Moshe Kahlon, Gideon Saar, and Silvan Shalom. And the opposition has failed to produce a credible alternative of its own. After leaving office in 2001, Barak undermined his standing by adopting a lavish lifestyle deemed unseemly for a Labor leader. Meanwhile, Tzipi Livni, Olmert's foreign minister and his successor as the head of Kadima, actually beat Netanyahu's Likud in the 2009 election, winning 28 seats to Likud's 27. But she was unable to build a large enough coalition to form the next government, and her subsequent weakness as opposition leader damaged her popular appeal.

Bennett is now trying to position himself as a younger and more populist version of his one-time mentor. There's no doubt that Bennett is charismatic and has grown quite popular. But he leads a small party with a limited base that cannot win an election unless it unites with Likud. Nir Barkat, the right-wing mayor of Jerusalem, is another former high- tech entrepreneur who harbors national aspirations. But he lacks charisma and remains unknown to the public outside Israel's capital city.

Netanyahu's strongest current challenger is probably Lapid, the former columnist and TV anchor who established Yesh Atid as a centrist party in 2012 and won a spectacular victory in 2013, earning Yesh Atid the second-highest number of seats in the Knesset. Lapid joined Netanyahu's cabinet after he and Bennett forced the prime minister to drop the ultra- Orthodox parties. But Netanyahu soon outmaneuvered him, pushing Lapid to the Treasury—a well-established graveyard for ambitious politicians, since it often involves making unpopular moves such as raising taxes and cutting benefits. Lapid accomplished little while in office, and in 2015, after a tough fight with Herzog and his Zionist Union over the same voters, Yesh Atid lost almost half its seats. Since then, Lapid has improved his public standing—popularity polls now put Yesh Atid second, after Likud—by appearing to be more religiously observant and by talking tough on terror. Lapid is a moderate (he supports a Palestinian state and opposes the expansion of remote West Bank settlements), is an excellent communicator, and is an astute reader of public sentiment. But he is hypersensitive—he tends to overreact when criticized—and he lacks security experience, a huge impediment in Israel.

None of this means that Netanyahu is invulnerable, however. In March, Haaretz published a poll showing that a new, imaginary centrist party led by Gabi Ashkenazi (a popular former IDF chief of staff), Kahlon, and Saar would beat Likud in an election held tomorrow. But unless its coalition crumbles, the government doesn't need to call a new election until November 2019, and the nonexistent party remains a fantasy. In the meantime, Netanyahu continues to maneuver. He has tried to entice the smaller right-wing parties into forming a new, broader party with Likud (so far, none of them has shown much interest). And this past spring, he held negotiations with Herzog over the formation of a unity coalition, only to back off at the last moment and offer his former ally Lieberman the post of defense minister. With Lieberman inside the government, the ruling coalition—more right-wing than ever—would get an expanded parliamentary base and more room to breathe.

Until the next election does come around, Netanyahu's government will keep trying to cement as many changes as possible to Israeli society and the Israeli establishment. The prime minister and his allies will push to appoint more conservatives to the Supreme Court and more religious Zionists to key government and academic positions. They will maintain their support for Mizrahi culture and West Bank settlements, will impose more restrictions on left-wing organ- izations, and will work to increase tensions with Israel's Arabs.

Regardless of who wins the next election, at least some of these changes seem likely to become permanent. The country has already become far less tolerant and open to debate than it used to be. The peace camp has withered, and very few really challenge the status of the occupation anymore. Arab- Jewish relations are so bad that they would take outstanding leadership and enormous effort to fix. And the United States' retrenchment has strengthened the sense among many Israelis that they can go it alone and no longer need to worry about pleasing Washington. It's hard to see how a new Israeli prime minister—or a new U.S. president—will be able to reverse many of these shifts.

ALUF BENN is Editor in Chief of *Haaretz*. Follow him on Twitter @alufbenn.

© Foreign Affairs

The Case for Offshore Balancing

A Superior U.S. Grand Strategy

John J. Mearsheimer and Stephen M. Walt

The amphibious assault ship USS Iwo Jima on the Hudson River in New York, May 2011.

For the first time in recent memory, large numbers of Americans are openly questioning their country's grand strategy. An April 2016 Pew poll found that 57 percent of Americans agree that the United States should "deal with its own problems and let others deal with theirs the best they can." On the campaign trail, both the Democrat Bernie Sanders and the Republican Donald Trump found receptive audiences whenever they questioned the United States' penchant for promoting democracy, subsidizing allies' defense, and intervening militarily—leaving only the likely Democratic nominee Hillary Clinton to defend the status quo.

Americans' distaste for the prevailing grand strategy should come as no surprise, given its abysmal record over the past quarter century. In Asia, India, Pakistan, and North Korea are expanding their nuclear arsenals, and China is challenging the status quo in regional waters. In Europe, Russia has annexed Crimea, and U.S. relations with Moscow have sunk to new lows since the Cold War. U.S. forces are still fighting in Afghanistan and Iraq, with no victory in sight. Despite losing most of its original leaders, al Qaeda has metastasized across the region. The Arab world has fallen into turmoil— in good part due to the United States' decisions to effect regime change in Iraq and Libya and its modest efforts to do the same in Syria—and the Islamic State, or ISIS, has emerged out of the chaos. Repeated U.S. attempts to broker Israeli-Palestinian peace have failed, leaving a two-state solution further away than ever. Meanwhile, democracy has been in retreat worldwide, and the United States' use of torture, targeted killings, and other morally dubious practices has tarnished its image as a defender of human rights and international law.

The United States does not bear sole responsibility for all these costly debacles, but it has had a hand in most of them. The setbacks are the natural consequence of the misguided grand strategy of liberal hegemony that Democrats and Republicans have pursued for years. This approach holds that the United States must use its power not only to solve global problems but also to promote a world order based on international institutions, representative governments, open markets, and respect for human rights. As "the indispensable nation," the logic goes, the United States has the right, responsibility, and wisdom to manage local politics almost everywhere. At its core, liberal hegemony is a revisionist grand strategy: instead of calling on the United States to merely uphold the balance of power in key regions, it commits American might to promoting democracy everywhere and defending human rights whenever they are threatened.

By husbanding U.S. strength, an offshore-balancing strategy would preserve U.S. primacy far into the future.

There is a better way. By pursuing a strategy of "offshore balancing," Washington would forgo ambitious efforts to remake other societies and concentrate on what really matters: preserving U.S. dominance in the Western Hemisphere and countering potential hegemons in Europe, Northeast Asia, and the Persian Gulf. Instead of policing the world, the United States would encourage other countries to take the lead in checking rising powers, intervening itself only when necessary. This does not mean abandoning the United States' position as the world's sole superpower or retreating to "Fortress America." Rather, by husbanding U.S. strength, offshore balancing would preserve U.S. primacy far into the future and safeguard liberty at home.

SETTING THE RIGHT GOALS

The United States is the luckiest great power in modern history. Other leading states have had to live with threatening adversaries in their own backyards—even the United Kingdom faced the prospect of an invasion from across the English Channel on several occasions—but for more than two centuries, the United States has not. Nor do distant powers pose much of a threat, because two giant oceans are in the way. As Jean-Jules Jusserand, the French ambassador to the United States from 1902 to 1924, once put it, "On the north, she has a weak neighbor; on the south, another weak neighbor; on the east, fish, and the west, fish." Furthermore, the United States boasts an abundance of land and natural resources and a large and energetic population, which have enabled it to develop the world's biggest economy and most capable military. It also has thousands of nuclear weapons, which makes an attack on the American homeland even less likely.

These geopolitical blessings give the United States enormous latitude for error; indeed, only a country as secure as it would have the temerity to try to remake the world in its own image. But they also allow it to remain powerful and secure without pursuing a costly and expansive grand strategy. Offshore balancing would do just that. Its principal concern would be to keep the United States as powerful as possible—ideally, the dominant state on the planet. Above all, that means main- taining hegemony in the Western Hemisphere.

Unlike isolationists, however, offshore balancers believe that there are regions outside the Western Hemisphere that are worth expending American blood and treasure to defend. Today, three other areas matter to the United States: Europe, Northeast Asia, and the Persian Gulf. The first two are key centers of industrial power and home to the world's other great powers, and the third produces roughly 30 percent of the world's oil.

In Europe and Northeast Asia, the chief concern is the rise of a regional hegemon that would dominate its region, much as the United States dominates the Western Hemisphere. Such a state would have abundant economic clout, the ability to develop sophisticated weaponry, the potential to project power around the globe, and perhaps even the wherewithal to outspend the United States in an arms race. Such a state might even ally with countries in the Western Hemisphere and interfere close to U.S. soil. Thus, the United States' principal aim in Europe and Northeast Asia should be to maintain the regional balance of power so that the most powerful state in each region—for now, Russia and China, respectively—remains too worried about its neighbors to roam into the Western Hemisphere. In the Gulf, meanwhile, the United States has an interest in blocking the rise of a hegemon that could interfere with the flow of oil from that region, thereby damaging the world economy and threatening U.S. prosperity.

Offshore balancing is a realist grand strategy, and its aims are limited. Promoting peace, although desirable, is not among them. This is not to say that Washington should welcome conflict anywhere in the world, or that it cannot use diplomatic or economic means to discourage war. But it should not commit U.S. military forces for that purpose alone. Nor is it a goal of offshore balancing to halt genocides, such as the one that befell Rwanda in 1994. Adopting this strategy would not preclude such operations, however, provided the need is clear, the mission is feasible, and U.S. leaders are confident that intervention will not make matters worse.

Chinese People's Liberation Army Navy members fire a salute during a commemoration ceremony for Chinese soldiers killed during the First Sino-Japanese War, near Liugong Island, China, August 2014.

HOW WOULD IT WORK?

Under offshore balancing, the United States would calibrate its military posture according to the distribution of power in the three key regions. If there is no potential hegemon in sight in Europe, Northeast Asia, or the Gulf, then there is no reason to deploy ground or air forces there and little need for a large military establishment at home. And because it takes many years for any country to acquire the capacity to dominate its region, Washington would see it coming and have time to respond.

In that event, the United States should turn to regional forces as the first line of defense, letting them uphold the balance of power in their own neighborhood. Although Washington could provide assistance to allies and pledge to support them if they were in danger of being conquered, it should refrain from deploying large numbers of U.S. forces abroad. It may occasionally make sense to keep certain assets overseas, such as small military contingents, intelligence-gathering facilities, or prepositioned equipment, but in general, Washington should pass the buck to regional powers, as they have a far greater interest in preventing any state from dominating them.

If those powers cannot contain a potential hegemon on their own, however, the United States must help get the job done, deploying enough firepower to the region to shift the balance in its favor. Sometimes, that may mean sending in forces before war breaks out. During the Cold War, for example, the United States kept large numbers of ground and air forces in Europe out of the belief that Western European countries could not contain the Soviet Union on their own. At other times, the United States might wait to intervene after a war starts, if one side seems likely to emerge as a regional hegemon. Such was the case during both world wars: the United States came in only after Germany seemed likely to dominate Europe.

In essence, the aim is to remain offshore as long as possible, while recognizing that it is sometimes necessary to come onshore. If that happens, however, the United States should make its allies do as much of the heavy lifting as possible and remove its own forces as soon as it can.

Offshore balancing has many virtues. By limiting the areas the U.S. military was committed to defending and forcing other states to pull their own weight, it would reduce the resources Washington must devote to defense, allow for greater investment and consumption at home, and put fewer American lives in harm's way. Today, allies routinely free-ride on American protection, a problem that has only grown since the Cold War ended. Within NATO, for example, the United States accounts for 46 percent of the alliance's aggregate GDP yet contributes about 75 percent of its military spending. As the political scientist Barry Posen has quipped, "This is welfare for the rich."

The aim is to remain offshore as long as possible, while recognizing that it is sometimes necessary to come onshore.

Offshore balancing would also reduce the risk of terrorism. Liberal hegemony commits the United States to spreading democracy in unfamiliar places, which sometimes requires military occupation and always involves interfering with local political arrangements. Such efforts invariably foster nationalist resentment, and because the opponents are too weak to confront the United States directly, they sometimes turn to terrorism. (It is worth remembering that Osama bin Laden was motivated in good part by the presence of U.S. troops in his homeland of Saudi Arabia.) In addition to inspiring terrorists, liberal hegemony facilitates their operations: using regime change to spread American values undermines local institutions and creates ungoverned spaces where violent extremists can flourish.

Offshore balancing would alleviate this problem by eschewing social engineering and minimizing the United States' military footprint. U.S. troops would be stationed on foreign soil only when a country was in a vital region and threatened by a would-be hegemon. In that case, the potential victim would view the United States as a savior rather than an occupier. And once the threat had been dealt with, U.S. military forces could go back over the horizon and not stay behind to meddle in local politics. By respecting the sovereignty of other states, offshore balancing would be less likely to foster anti-American terrorism.

A REASSURING HISTORY

Offshore balancing may seem like a radical strategy today, but it provided the guiding logic of U.S. foreign policy for many decades and served the country well. During the nineteenth century, the United States was preoccupied with expanding across North America, building a powerful state, and establishing hegemony in the Western Hemisphere. After it completed these tasks at the end of the century, it soon became interested in preserving the balance of power in Europe and Northeast Asia. Nonetheless, it let the great powers in those regions check one another, intervening militarily only when the balance of power broke down, as during both world wars.

During the Cold War, the United States had no choice but to go onshore in Europe and Northeast Asia, as its allies in those regions could not contain the Soviet Union by themselves. So Washington forged alliances and stationed military forces in both regions, and it fought the Korean War to contain Soviet influence in Northeast Asia.

In the Persian Gulf, however, the United States stayed offshore, letting the United Kingdom take the lead in preventing any state from dominating that oil-rich region. After the British announced their withdrawal from the Gulf in 1968, the United States turned to the shah of Iran and the Saudi monarchy to do the job. When the shah fell in 1979, the Carter administration began building the Rapid Deployment Force, an offshore military capability designed to prevent Iran or the Soviet Union from dominating the region. The Reagan administration aided Iraq during that country's 1980–88 war with Iran for similar reasons. The U.S. military stayed offshore until 1990, when Saddam Hussein's seizure of Kuwait threatened to enhance Iraq's power and place Saudi Arabia and other Gulf oil producers at risk. To restore the regional balance of power, the George H. W. Bush admin- istration sent an expeditionary force to liberate Kuwait and smash Saddam's military machine.

For nearly a century, in short, offshore balancing prevented the emergence of dangerous regional hegemons and pre- served a global balance of power that enhanced American security. Tellingly, when U.S. policymakers deviated from that strategy—as they did in Vietnam, where the United States had no vital interests—the result was a costly failure.

Events since the end of the Cold War teach the same lesson. In Europe, once the Soviet Union collapsed, the region no longer had a dominant power. The United States should have steadily reduced its military presence, cultivated amicable relations with Russia, and turned European security over to the Europeans. Instead, it expanded NATO and ignored Russian interests, helping spark the conflict over Ukraine and driving Moscow closer to China.

In the Middle East, likewise, the United States should have moved back offshore after the Gulf War and let Iran and Iraq balance each other. Instead, the Clinton administration adopted the policy of "dual containment," which required keeping ground and air forces in Saudi Arabia to check Iran and Iraq simultaneously. The George W. Bush administration then adopted an even more ambitious strategy, dubbed "regional transformation," which produced costly failures in Afghanistan and Iraq. The Obama administration repeated the error when it helped topple Muammar al-Qaddafi in Libya and when it exacerbated the chaos in Syria by insisting that Bashar al-Assad "must go" and backing some of his opponents. Abandoning offshore balancing after the Cold War has been a recipe for failure.

HEGEMONY'S HOLLOW HOPES

Defenders of liberal hegemony marshal a number of unpersuasive arguments to make their case. One familiar claim is that only vigorous U.S. leadership can keep order around the globe. But global leadership is not an end in itself; it is desirable only insofar as it benefits the United States directly.

One might further argue that U.S. leadership is necessary to overcome the collective-action problem of local actors failing to balance against a potential hegemon. Offshore balancing recognizes this danger, however, and calls for Washington to step in if needed. Nor does it prohibit Washington from giving friendly states in the key regions advice or material aid.

Other defenders of liberal hegemony argue that U.S. leadership is necessary to deal with new, transnational threats that arise from failed states, terrorism, criminal networks, refugee flows, and the like. Not only do the Atlantic and Pacific Oceans offer inadequate protection against these dangers, they claim, but modern military technology also makes it easier for the United States to project power around the world and address them. Today's "global village," in short, is more dangerous yet easier to manage.

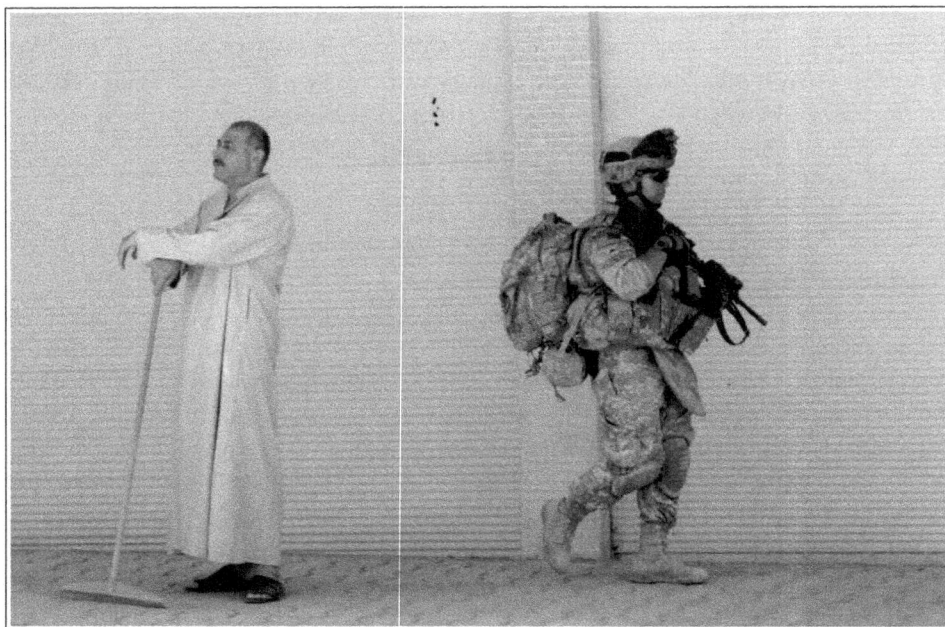

A U.S. soldier walks past a resident during a patrol in Samarra, Iraq, June 2009.

This view exaggerates these threats and overstates Washington's ability to eliminate them. Crime, terrorism, and similar problems can be a nuisance, but they are hardly existential threats and rarely lend themselves to military solutions. Indeed, constant interference in the affairs of other states—and especially repeated military interventions—generates local resentment and fosters corruption, thereby making these transnational dangers worse. The long-term solution to the problems can only be competent local governance, not heavy-handed U.S. efforts to police the world.

Nor is policing the world as cheap as defenders of liberal hegemony contend, either in dollars spent or in lives lost. The wars in Afghanistan and Iraq cost between $4 trillion and $6 trillion and killed nearly 7,000 U.S. soldiers and wounded more than 50,000. Veterans of these conflicts exhibit high rates of depression and suicide, yet the United States has little to show for their sacrifices.

Defenders of the status quo also fear that offshore balancing would allow other states to replace the United States at the pinnacle of global power. On the contrary, the strategy would prolong the country's dominance by refocusing its efforts on core goals. Unlike liberal hegemony, offshore balancing avoids squandering resources on costly and counterproductive crusades, which would allow the government to invest more in the long-term ingredients of power and prosperity: education, infrastructure, and research and development. Remember, the United States became a great power by staying out of foreign wars and building a world-class economy, which is the same strategy China has pursued over the past three decades. Meanwhile, the United States has wasted trillions of dollars and put its long-term primacy at risk.

Another argument holds that the U.S. military must garrison the world to keep the peace and preserve an open world economy. Retrenchment, the logic goes, would renew great- power competition, invite ruinous economic rivalries, and eventually spark a major war from which the United States could not remain aloof. Better to keep playing global policeman than risk a repeat of the 1930s.

Such fears are unconvincing. For starters, this argument assumes that deeper U.S. engagement in Europe would have prevented World War II, a claim hard to square with Adolf Hitler's unshakable desire for war. Regional conflicts will sometimes occur no matter what Washington does, but it need not get involved unless vital U.S. interests are at stake. Indeed, the United States has sometimes stayed out of regional conflicts—such as the Russo-Japanese War, the Iran- Iraq War, and the current war in Ukraine—belying the claim that it inevitably gets dragged in. And if the country is forced to fight another great power, better to arrive late and let other countries bear the brunt of the costs. As the last major power to enter both world wars, the United States emerged stronger from each for having waited.

Furthermore, recent history casts doubt on the claim that U.S. leadership preserves peace. Over the past 25 years, Washington has caused or supported several wars in the Middle East and fueled minor conflicts elsewhere. If liberal hegemony is supposed to enhance global stability, it has done a poor job.

Nor has the strategy produced much in the way of economic benefits. Given its protected position in the Western Hemisphere, the United States is free to trade and invest wherever profitable opportunities exist. Because all countries have a shared interest in such activity, Washington does not need to play global policeman in order to remain economically engaged with others. In fact, the U.S. economy would be in better shape today if the government were not spending so much money trying to run the world.

Offshore balancing may seem like a radical strategy today, but it provided the guiding logic of U.S. foreign policy for many decades.

Proponents of liberal hegemony also claim that the United States must remain committed all over the world to prevent nuclear proliferation. If it reduces its role in key regions or withdraws entirely, the argument runs, countries accustomed to U.S. protection will have no choice but to protect themselves by obtaining nuclear weapons.

No grand strategy is likely to prove wholly successful at preventing proliferation, but offshore balancing would do a better job than liberal hegemony. After all, that strategy failed to stop India and Pakistan from ramping up their nuclear capabilities, North Korea from becoming the newest member of the nuclear club, and Iran from making major progress with its nuclear program. Countries usually seek the bomb because they fear being attacked, and U.S. efforts at regime change only heighten such concerns. By eschewing regime change and reducing the United States' military footprint, offshore balancing would give potential proliferators less reason to go nuclear.

Moreover, military action cannot prevent a determined country from eventually obtaining nuclear weapons; it can only buy time. The recent deal with Iran serves as a reminder that coordinated multilateral pressure and tough economic sanctions are a better way to discourage proliferation than preventive war or regime change.

To be sure, if the United States did scale back its security guarantees, a few vulnerable states might seek their own nuclear deterrents. That outcome is not desirable, but all-out efforts to prevent it would almost certainly be costly and probably be unsuccessful. Besides, the downsides may not be as grave as pessimists fear. Getting the bomb does not transform weak countries into great powers or enable them to blackmail rival states. Ten states have crossed the nuclear threshold since 1945, and the world has not turned upside down. Nuclear proliferation will remain a concern no matter what the United States does, but offshore balancing provides the best strategy for dealing with it.

THE DEMOCRACY DELUSION

Other critics reject offshore balancing because they believe the United States has a moral and strategic imperative to promote freedom and protect human rights. As they see it, spreading democracy will largely rid the world of war and atrocities, keeping the United States secure and alleviating suffering.

No one knows if a world composed solely of liberal democracies would in fact prove peaceful, but spreading democracy at the point of a gun rarely works, and fledgling democracies are especially prone to conflict. Instead of promoting peace, the United States just ends up fighting endless wars. Even worse, force-feeding liberal values abroad can compromise them at home. The global war on terrorism and the related effort to implant democracy in Afghanistan and Iraq have led to tortured prisoners, targeted killings, and vast electronic surveillance of U.S. citizens.

Some defenders of liberal hegemony hold that a subtler version of the strategy could avoid the sorts of disasters that occurred in Afghanistan, Iraq, and Libya. They are deluding themselves. Democracy promotion requires large-scale social engineering in foreign societies that Americans understand poorly, which helps explain why Washington's efforts usually fail. Dismantling and replacing existing political institutions inevitably creates winners and losers, and the latter often take up arms in opposition. When that happens, U.S. officials, believing their country's credibility is now at stake, are tempted to use the United States' awesome military might to fix the problem, thus drawing the country into more conflicts.

If the American people want to encourage the spread of liberal democracy, the best way to do so is to set a good example. Other countries will more likely emulate the United States if they see it as a just, prosperous, and open society. And that means doing more to improve conditions at home and less to manipulate politics abroad.

THE PROBLEMATIC PACIFIER

Then there are those who believe that Washington should reject liberal hegemony but keep sizable U.S. forces in Europe, Northeast Asia, and the Persian Gulf solely to prevent trouble from breaking out. This low-cost insurance policy, they argue, would save lives and money in the long run, because the United States wouldn't have to ride to the rescue after a conflict broke out. This approach—sometimes called "selective engagement"—sounds appealing but would not work either.

For starters, it would likely revert back to liberal hegemony. Once committed to preserving peace in key regions, U.S. leaders would be sorely tempted to spread democracy, too, based on the widespread belief that democracies don't fight one another. This was the main rationale for expanding NATO after the Cold War, with the stated goal of "a Europe whole and free." In the real world, the line separating selective engagement from liberal hegemony is easily erased.

There is no good reason to keep U.S. forces in Europe, as no country there has the capability to dominate that region.

Advocates of selective engagement also assume that the mere presence of U.S. forces in various regions will guarantee peace, and so Americans need not worry about being dragged into distant conflicts. In other words, extending security commitments far and wide poses few risks, because they will never have to be honored.

But this assumption is overly optimistic: allies may act recklessly, and the United States may provoke conflicts itself. Indeed, in Europe, the American pacifier failed to prevent the Balkan wars of the 1990s, the Russo-Georgian war in 2008, and the current conflict in Ukraine. In the Middle East, Washington is largely responsible for several recent wars. And in the South China Sea, conflict is now a real possibility despite the U.S. Navy's substantial regional role. Stationing U.S. forces around the world does not automatically ensure peace.

Nor does selective engagement address the problem of buck-passing. Consider that the United Kingdom is now withdrawing its army from continental Europe, at a time when NATO faces what it considers a growing threat from Russia. Once again, Washington is expected to deal with the problem, even though peace in Europe should matter far more to the region's own powers.

THE STRATEGY IN ACTION

What would offshore balancing look like in today's world? The good news is that it is hard to foresee a serious challenge to American hegemony in the Western Hemisphere, and for now, no potential hegemon lurks in Europe or the Persian Gulf. Now for the bad news: if China continues its impressive rise, it is likely to seek hegemony in Asia. The United States should undertake a major effort to prevent it from succeeding.

Ideally, Washington would rely on local powers to contain China, but that strategy might not work. Not only is China likely to be much more powerful than its neighbors, but these states are also located far from one another, making it harder to form an effective balancing coalition. The United States will have to coordinate their efforts and may have to throw its considerable weight behind them. In Asia, the United States may indeed be the indispensable nation.

In Europe, the United States should end its military presence and turn NATO over to the Europeans. There is no good reason to keep U.S. forces in Europe, as no country there has the capability to dominate that region. The top contenders, Germany and Russia, will both lose relative power as their populations shrink in size, and no other potential hegemon is in sight. Admittedly, leaving European security to the Europeans could increase the potential for trouble there. If a conflict did arise, however, it would not threaten vital U.S. interests. Thus, there is no reason for the United States to spend billions of dollars each year (and pledge its own citizens' lives) to prevent one.

In the Gulf, the United States should return to the offshore- balancing strategy that served it so well until the advent of dual containment. No local power is now in a position to dominate the region, so the United States can move most of its forces back over the horizon.

With respect to ISIS, the United States should let the regional powers deal with that group and limit its own efforts to providing arms, intelligence, and military training. ISIS represents a serious threat to them but a minor problem for the United States, and the only long-term solution to it is better local institutions, something Washington cannot provide.

In Syria, the United States should let Russia take the lead. A Syria stabilized under Assad's control, or divided into competing ministates, would pose little danger to U.S. interests. Both Democratic and Republican presidents have a rich history of working with the Assad regime, and a divided and weak Syria would not threaten the regional balance of power. If the civil war continues, it will be largely Moscow's problem, although Washington should be willing to help broker a political settlement.

For now, the United States should pursue better relations with Iran. It is not in Washington's interest for Tehran to abandon the nuclear agreement and race for the bomb, an outcome that would become more likely if it feared a U.S. attack—hence the rationale for mending fences. Moreover, as its ambitions grow, China will want allies in the Gulf, and Iran will likely top its list. (In a harbinger of things to come, this past January, Chinese President Xi Jinping visited Tehran and signed 17 different agreements.) The United States has an obvious interest in discouraging Chinese-Iranian security cooperation, and that requires reaching out to Iran.

Iran has a significantly larger population and greater economic potential than its Arab neighbors, and it may eventually be in a position to dominate the Gulf. If it begins to move in this direction, the United States should help the other Gulf states balance against Tehran, calibrating its own efforts and regional military presence to the magnitude of the danger.

THE BOTTOM LINE

Taken together, these steps would allow the United States to markedly reduce its defense spending. Although U.S. forces would remain in Asia, the withdrawals from Europe and the Persian Gulf would free up billions of dollars, as would reductions in counterterrorism spending and an end to the war in Afghanistan and other overseas interventions. The United States would maintain substantial naval and air assets and modest but capable ground forces, and it would stand ready to expand its capabilities should circumstances require. But for the foreseeable future, the U.S. government could spend more money on domestic needs or leave it in taxpayers' pockets.

Offshore balancing is a grand strategy born of confidence in the United States' core traditions and a recognition of its enduring advantages. It exploits the country's providential geographic position and recognizes the powerful incentives other states have to balance against overly powerful or ambitious neighbors. It respects the power of nationalism, does not try to impose American values on foreign societies, and focuses on setting an example that others will want to emulate. As in the past, offshore balancing is not only the strategy that hews closest to U.S. interests; it is also the one that aligns best with Americans' preferences.

JOHN J. MEARSHEIMER is R. Wendell Harrison Distinguished Service Professor of Political Science at the University of Chicago. STEPHEN M. WALT is Robert and Renée Belfer Professor of International Affairs at the Harvard Kennedy School. Follow him on Twitter @StephenWalt.

The Truth About Trade

What Critics Get Wrong About the Global Economy

Douglas A. Irwin

A container ship enters New York Harbor, November 2015.

Just because a U.S. presidential candidate bashes free trade on the campaign trail does not mean that he or she cannot embrace it once elected. After all, Barack Obama voted against the Central American Free Trade Agreement as a U.S. senator and disparaged the North American Free Trade Agreement (NAFTA) as a presidential candidate. In office, however, he came to champion the Trans-Pacific Partnership (TPP), a giant trade deal with 11 other Pacific Rim countries. Yet in the current election cycle, the rhetorical attacks on U.S. trade policy have grown so fiery that it is difficult to imagine similar transformations. The Democratic candidate Bernie Sanders has railed against "disastrous" trade agreements, which he claims have cost jobs and hurt the middle class. The Republican Donald Trump complains that China, Japan, and Mexico are "killing" the United States on trade thanks to the bad deals struck by "stupid" negotiators. Even Hillary Clinton, the expected Democratic nominee, who favored the TPP as secretary of state, has been forced to join the chorus and now says she opposes that agreement.

Blaming other countries for the United States' economic woes is an age-old tradition in American politics; if truth is the first casualty of war, then support for free trade is often an early casualty of an election campaign. But the bipartisan bombardment has been so intense this time, and has been so unopposed, that it raises real questions about the future of U.S. global economic leadership.

The anti-trade rhetoric paints a grossly distorted picture of trade's role in the U.S. economy. Trade still benefits the United States enormously, and striking back at other countries by imposing new barriers or ripping up existing agreements would be self-destructive. The badmouthing of trade agreements has even jeopardized the ratification of the TPP in Congress. Backing out of that deal would signal a major U.S. retreat from Asia and mark a historic error.

Still, it would be a mistake to dismiss all of the anti-trade talk as ill-informed bombast. Today's electorate harbors legitimate, deep-seated frustrations about the state of the U.S. economy and labor markets in particular, and addressing these complaints will require changing government policies. The solution, however, lies not in turning away from trade promotion but in strengthening worker protections.

By and large, the United States has no major difficulties with respect to trade, nor does it suffer from problems that could be solved by trade barriers. What it does face, however, is a much larger problem, one that lies at the root of anxieties over trade: the economic ladder that allowed previous generations of lower-skilled Americans to reach the middle class is broken.

SCAPEGOATING TRADE

Campaign attacks on trade leave an unfortunate impression on the American public and the world at large. In saying that some countries "win" and other countries "lose" as a result of trade, for example, Trump portrays it as a zero-sum game. That's an understandable perspective for a casino owner and businessman: gambling is the quintessential zero-sum game, and competition is a win-lose proposition for firms (if not for their customers). But it is dead wrong as a way to think about the role of trade in an economy. Trade is actually a two-way street—the exchange of exports for imports— that makes efficient use of a country's resources to increase its material welfare. The United States sells to other countries the goods and services that it produces relatively efficiently (from aircraft to soybeans to legal advice) and buys those goods and services that other countries produce relatively efficiently (from T-shirts to bananas to electronics assembly). In the aggregate, both sides benefit.

To make their case that trade isn't working for the United States, critics invoke long-discredited indicators, such as the country's negative balance of trade. "Our trade deficit with China is like having a business that continues to lose money every single year," Trump once said. "Who would do business like that?" In fact, a nation's trade balance is nothing like a firm's bottom line. Whereas a company cannot lose money indefinitely, a country—particularly one, such as the United States, with a reserve currency—can run a trade deficit indefinitely without compromising its well-being. Australia has run current account deficits even longer than the United States has, and its economy is flourishing.

One way to define a country's trade balance is the difference between its domestic savings and its domestic investment. The United States has run a deficit in its current account—the broadest measure of trade in goods and services—every year except one since 1981. Why? Because as a low-saving, high- consuming country, the United States has long been the recipient of capital inflows from abroad. Reducing the current account deficit would require foreigners to purchase fewer U.S assets. That, in turn, would require increasing domestic savings or, to put it in less popular terms, reducing consumption. One way to accomplish that would be to change the tax system—for example, by instituting a consumption tax. But discouraging spending and rewarding savings is not easy, and critics of the trade deficit do not fully appreciate the difficulty involved in reversing it. (And if a current account surplus were to appear, critics would no doubt complain, as they did in the 1960s, that the United States was investing too much abroad and not enough at home.)

Trade still benefits the United States enormously.

Critics also point to the trade deficit to suggest that the United States is losing more jobs as a result of imports than it gains due to exports. In fact, the trade deficit usually increases when the economy is growing and creating jobs and decreases when it is contracting and losing jobs. The U.S. current account deficit shrank from 5.8 percent of GDP in 2006 to 2.7 percent in 2009, but that didn't stop the economy from hemorrhaging jobs. And if there is any doubt that a current account surplus is no economic panacea, one need only look at Japan, which has endured three decades of economic stagnation despite running consistent current account surpluses.

And yet these basic fallacies—many of which Adam Smith debunked more than two centuries ago—have found a new life in contemporary American politics. In some ways, it is odd that anti-trade sentiment has blossomed in 2016, of all years. For one thing, although the post-recession recovery has been disappointing, it has hardly been awful: the U.S. economy has experienced seven years of slow but steady growth, and the unemployment rate has fallen to just five percent. For another thing, imports have not swamped the country and caused problems for domestic producers and their workers; over the past seven years, the current account deficit has remained roughly unchanged at about two to three percent of GDP, much lower than its level from 2000 to 2007. The pace of globalization, meanwhile, has slowed in recent years. The World Trade Organization (WTO) forecasts that the volume of world trade will grow by just 2.8 percent in 2016, the fifth consecutive year that it has grown by less than three percent, down significantly from previous decades.

Nice work if you can get it: at a Ford plant in Michigan, November 2012.

What's more, despite what one might infer from the crowds at campaign rallies, Americans actually support foreign trade in general and even trade agreements such as the TPP in particular. After a decade of viewing trade with skepticism, since 2013, Americans have seen it positively. A February 2016 Gallup poll found that 58 percent of Americans consider foreign trade an opportunity for economic growth, and only 34 percent viewed it as a threat.

THE VIEW FROM THE BOTTOM

So why has trade come under such strident attack now? The most important reason is that workers are still suffering from the aftermath of the Great Recession, which left many unemployed and indebted. Between 2007 and 2009, the United States lost nearly nine million jobs, pushing the unemployment rate up to ten percent. Seven years later, the economy is still recovering from this devastating blow. Many workers have left the labor force, reducing the employment- to-population ratio sharply. Real wages have remained flat. For many Americans, the recession isn't over.

For many Americans, the recession isn't over.

Thus, even as trade commands broad public support, a significant minority of the electorate—about a third, according to various polls—decidedly opposes it. These critics come from both sides of the political divide, but they tend to be lower-income, blue-collar workers, who are the most vulnerable to economic change. They believe that economic elites and the political establishment have looked out only for themselves over the past few decades. As they see it, the government bailed out banks during the financial crisis, but no one came to their aid.

For these workers, neither political party has taken their concerns seriously, and both parties have struck trade deals that the workers think have cost jobs. Labor unions that support the Democrats still feel betrayed by President Bill Clinton, who, over their strong objections, secured congressional passage of NAFTA in 1993 and normalized trade relations with China in 2000. Blue-collar Republican voters, for their part, supported the anti-NAFTA presidential campaigns of Pat Buchanan and Ross Perot in 1992. They felt betrayed by President George W. Bush, who pushed Congress to pass many bilateral trade agreements. Today, they back Trump.

Among this demographic, a narrative has taken hold that trade has cost Americans their jobs, squeezed the middle class, and kept wages low. The truth is more complicated. Although imports have put some people out of work, trade is far from the most important factor behind the loss of manufacturing jobs. The main culprit is technology. Auto- mation and other technologies have enabled vast productivity and efficiency improvements, but they have also made many blue-collar jobs obsolete. One representative study, by the Center for Business and Economic Research at Ball State University, found that productivity growth accounted for more than 85 percent of the job loss in manufacturing between 2000 and 2010, a period when employment in that sector fell by 5.6 million. Just 13 percent of the overall job loss resulted from trade, although in two sectors, apparel and furniture, it accounted for 40 percent.

This finding is consistent with research by the economists David Autor, David Dorn, and Gordon Hanson, who have estimated that imports from China displaced as many as 982,000 workers in manufacturing from 2000 to 2007. These layoffs also depressed local labor markets in communities that produced goods facing Chinese competition, such as textiles, apparel, and furniture. The number of jobs lost is large, but it should be put in perspective: while Chinese imports may have cost nearly one million manufacturing jobs over almost a decade, the normal churn of U.S. labor markets results in roughly 1.7 million layoffs every month.

Robotic arms work on the chassis of a Ford Transit Van at the Ford Claycomo Assembly Plant in Claycomo, Missouri, April 2014.

Research into the effect of Chinese imports on U.S. employment has been widely misinterpreted to imply that the United States has gotten a raw deal from trade with China. In fact, such studies do not evaluate the gains from trade, since they make no attempt to quantify the benefits to consumers from lower-priced goods. Rather, they serve as a reminder that a rapid increase in imports can harm communities that produce substitute goods—as happened in the U.S. automotive and steel sectors in the 1980s.

Furthermore, the shock of Chinese goods was a one-time event that occurred under special circumstances. Imports from China increased from 1.0 percent of U.S. GDP in 2000 to 2.6 percent in 2011, but for the past five years, the share has stayed roughly constant. There is no reason to believe it will rise further. China's once-rapid economic growth has slowed. Its working-age population has begun to shrink, and the migration of its rural workers to coastal urban manufacturing areas has largely run its course.

The influx of Chinese imports was also unusual in that much of it occurred from 2001 to 2007, when China's current account surplus soared, reaching ten percent of GDP in 2007. The country's export boom was partly facilitated by China's policy of preventing the appreciation of the yuan, which lowered the price of Chinese goods. Beginning around 2000, the Chinese central bank engaged in a large-scale, persistent, and one-way intervention in the foreign exchange market—buying dollars and selling yuan. As a result, its foreign exchange reserves rose from less than $300 million in 2000 to $3.25 trillion in 2011. Critics rightly groused that this effort constituted currency manipulation and violated International Monetary Fund rules. Yet such complaints are now moot: over the past year, China's foreign exchange reserves have fallen rapidly as its central bank has sought to prop up the value of the yuan. Punishing China for past bad behavior would accomplish nothing.

THE RIGHT—AND WRONG—SOLUTIONS

The real problem is not trade but diminished domestic opportunity and social mobility. Although the United States boasts a highly skilled work force and a solid technological base, it is still the case that only one in three American adults has a college education. In past decades, the two-thirds of Americans with no postsecondary degree often found work in manufacturing, construction, or the armed forces. These parts of the economy stood ready to absorb large numbers of people with limited education, give them productive work, and help them build skills. Over time, however, these opportunities have disappeared. Technology has shrunk manufacturing as a source of large-scale employment: even though U.S. manufacturing output continues to grow, it does so with many fewer workers than in the past. Construction work has not recovered from the bursting of the housing bubble. And the military turns away 80 percent of applicants due to stringent fitness and intelligence requirements. There are no comparable sectors of the economy that can employ large numbers of high-school-educated workers.

The anti-trade rhetoric of the campaign has made it difficult for even pro-trade members of Congress to support new agreements.

This is a deep problem for American society. The unemployment rate for college-educated workers is 2.4 percent, but it is more than 7.4 percent for those without a high school diploma—and even higher when counting discouraged workers who have left the labor force but wish to work. These are the people who have been left behind in the twenty-first-century economy—again, not primarily because of trade but because of structural changes in the economy. Helping these workers and ensuring that the economy delivers benefits to everyone should rank as urgent priorities.

But here is where the focus on trade is a diversion. Since trade is not the underlying problem in terms of job loss, neither is protectionism a solution. While the gains from trade can seem abstract, the costs of trade restrictions are concrete. For example, the United States has some 135,000 workers employed in the apparel industry, but there are more than 45 million Americans who live below the poverty line, stretching every dollar they have. Can one really justify increasing the price of clothing for 45 million low-income Americans (and everyone else as well) in an effort to save the jobs of just some of the 135,000 low-wage workers in the apparel industry?

Like undoing trade agreements, imposing selective import duties to punish specific countries would also fail. If the United States were to slap 45 percent tariffs on imports from China, as Trump has proposed, U.S. companies would not start producing more apparel and footwear in the United States, nor would they start assembling consumer electronics domestically. Instead, production would shift from China to other low-wage developing countries in Asia, such as Vietnam. That's the lesson of past trade sanctions directed against China alone: in 2009, when the Obama administration imposed duties on automobile tires from China in an effort to save American jobs, other suppliers, principally Indonesia and Thailand, filled the void, resulting in little impact on U.S. production or jobs.

And if restrictions were levied against all foreign imports to prevent such trade diversion, those barriers would hit innocent bystanders: Canada, Japan, Mexico, the EU, and many others. Any number of these would use WTO procedures to retaliate against the United States, threatening the livelihoods of the millions of Americans with jobs that depend on exports of manufactured goods. Trade wars produce no winners. There are good reasons why the very mention of the 1930 Smoot-Hawley Tariff Act still conjures up memories of the Great Depression.

Ripping up NAFTA would do immense damage.

If protectionism is an ineffectual and counterproductive response to the economic problems of much of the work force, so, too, are existing programs designed to help workers displaced by trade. The standard package of Trade Adjustment Assistance, a federal program begun in the 1960s, consists of extended unemployment compensation and retraining programs. But because these benefits are limited to workers who lost their jobs due to trade, they miss the millions more who are unemployed on account of technological change. Furthermore, the program is fraught with bad incentives. Extended unemployment compensation pays workers for prolonged periods of joblessness, but their job prospects usually deteriorate the longer they stay out of the labor force, since they have lost experience in the interim.

And although the idea behind retraining is a good one—helping laid-off textile or steel workers become nurses or technicians—the actual program is a failure. A 2012 external review commissioned by the Department of Labor found that the government retraining programs were a net loss for society, to the tune of about $54,000 per participant. Half of that fell on the participants themselves, who, on average, earned

$27,000 less over the four years of the study than similar workers who did not find jobs through the program, and half fell on the government, which footed the bill for the program. Sadly, these programs appear to do more harm than good.

A better way to help all low-income workers would be to expand the Earned Income Tax Credit. The EITC supplements the incomes of workers in all low-income households, not just those the Department of Labor designates as having been adversely affected by trade. What's more, the EITC is tied to employment, thereby rewarding work and keeping people in the labor market, where they can gain experience and build skills. A large enough EITC could ensure that every American was able to earn the equivalent of $15 or more per hour. And it could do so without any of the job loss that a minimum-wage hike can cause. Of all the potential assistance programs, the EITC also enjoys the most bipartisan support, having been endorsed by both the Obama administration and Paul Ryan, the Republican Speaker of the House. A higher EITC would not be a cure-all, but it would provide income security for those seeking to climb the ladder to the middle class.

The main complaint about expanding the EITC concerns the cost. Yet taxpayers are already bearing the burden of supporting workers who leave the labor force, many of whom start receiving disability payments. On disability, people are paid—permanently—to drop out of the labor force and not work. In lieu of this federal program, the cost of which has surged in recent years, it would be better to help people remain in the work force through the EITC, in the hope that they can eventually become taxpayers themselves.

THE FUTURE OF FREE TRADE

Despite all the evidence of the benefits of trade, many of this year's crop of presidential candidates have still invoked it as a bogeyman. Sanders deplores past agreements but has yet to clarify whether he believes that better ones could have been negotiated or no such agreements should be reached at all. His vote against the U.S.-Australian free-trade agreement in 2004 suggests that he opposes all trade deals, even one with a country that has high labor standards and with which the United States runs a sizable balance of trade surplus. Trump professes to believe in free trade, but he insists that the United States has been outnegotiated by its trade partners, hence his threat to impose 45 percent tariffs on imports from China to get "a better deal"—whatever that means. He has attacked Japan's barriers against imports of U.S. agricultural goods, even though that is exactly the type of protectionism the TPP has tried to undo. Meanwhile, Clinton's position against the TPP has hardened as the campaign has gone on.

The response from economists has tended to be either meek defenses of trade or outright silence, with some even criticizing parts of the TPP. It's time for supporters of free trade to engage in a full-throated championing of the many achievements of U.S. trade agreements. Indeed, because other countries' trade barriers tend to be higher than those of the United States, trade agreements open foreign markets to U.S. exports more than they open the U.S. market to foreign imports.

A worker stands next to shipping containers on a ship at a port in Bangkok, Thailand, March 2016.

That was true of NAFTA, which remains a favored punching bag on the campaign trail. In fact, NAFTA has been a big economic and foreign policy success. Since the agreement entered into force in 1994, bilateral trade between the United States and Mexico has boomed. For all the fear about Mexican imports flooding the U.S. market, it is worth noting that about 40 percent of the value of imports from Mexico consists of content originally made in the United States—for example, auto parts produced in the United States but assembled in Mexico. It is precisely such trade in component parts that makes standard measures of bilateral trade balances so misleading.

NAFTA has also furthered the United States' long-term political, diplomatic, and economic interest in a flourishing, democratic Mexico, which not only reduces immigration pressures on border states but also increases Mexican demand for U.S. goods and services. Far from exploiting Third World labor, as critics have charged, NAFTA has promoted the growth of a middle class in Mexico that now includes nearly half of all households. And since 2009, more Mexicans have left the United States than have come in. In the two decades since NAFTA went into effect, Mexico has been transformed from a clientelistic one-party state with widespread anti-American sentiment into a functional multiparty democracy with a generally pro-American public. Although it has suffered from drug wars in recent years (a spillover effect from problems that are largely made in America), the overall story is one of rising prosperity thanks in part to NAFTA.

Ripping up NAFTA would do immense damage. In its foreign relations, the United States would prove itself to be an unreliable partner. And economically, getting rid of the agreement would disrupt production chains across North America, harming both Mexico and the United States. It would add to border tensions while shifting trade to Asia without bringing back any U.S. manufacturing jobs. The American public seems to understand this: in an October 2015 Gallup poll, only 18 percent of respondents agreed that leaving NAFTA or the Central American Free Trade Agreement would be very effective in helping the economy.

A more moderate option would be for the United States to take a pause and simply stop negotiating any more trade agreements, as Obama did during his first term. The problem with this approach, however, is that the rest of the world would continue to reach trade agreements without the United States, and so U.S. exporters would find themselves at a disadvantage compared with their foreign competitors. Glimpses of that future can already be seen. In 2012, the car manufacturer Audi chose southeastern Mexico over Tennessee for the site of a new plant because it could save thousands of dollars per car exported thanks to Mexico's many more free-trade agreements, including one with the EU. Australia has reached trade deals with China and Japan that give Australian farmers preferential access in those markets, cutting into U.S. beef exports.

If Washington opted out of the TPP, it would forgo an opportunity to shape the rules of international trade in the twenty-first century. The Uruguay Round, the last round of international trade negotiations completed by the General Agreement on Tariffs and Trade, ended in 1994, before the Internet had fully emerged. Now, the United States' high-tech firms and other exporters face foreign regulations that are not transparent and impede market access. Meanwhile, other countries are already moving ahead with their own trade agreements, increasingly taking market share from U.S. exporters in the dynamic Asia-Pacific region. Staying out of the TPP would not lead to the creation of good jobs in the United States. And despite populist claims to the contrary, the TPP's provisions for settling disputes between investors and governments and dealing with intellectual property rights are reasonable. (In the early 1990s, similar fears about such provisions in the WTO were just as exaggerated and ultimately proved baseless.)

The United States should proceed with passage of the TPP and continue to negotiate other deals with its trading partners. So-called plurilateral trade agreements, that is, deals among relatively small numbers of like-minded countries, offer the only viable way to pick up more gains from reducing trade barriers. The current climate on Capitol Hill means that the era of small bilateral agreements, such as those pursued during the George W. Bush administration, has ended. And the collapse of the Doha Round at the WTO likely marks the end of giant multilateral trade negotiations.

Free trade has always been a hard sell. But the anti-trade rhetoric of the 2016 campaign has made it difficult for even pro-trade members of Congress to support new agreements. Past experience suggests that Washington will lead the charge for reducing trade barriers only when there is a major trade problem to be solved—namely, when U.S. exporters face severe discrimination in foreign markets. Such was the case when the United States helped form the General Agreement on Tariffs and Trade in 1947, when it started the Kennedy Round of trade negotiations in the 1960s, and when it initiated the Uruguay Round in the 1980s. Until the United States feels the pain of getting cut out of major foreign markets, its leadership on global trade may wane. That would represent just one casualty of the current campaign.

DOUGLAS A. IRWIN is John Sloan Dickey Third Century Professor in the Social Sciences in the Department of Economics at Dartmouth College and the author of *Free Trade Under Fire*. Follow him on Twitter @D_A_Irwin.

France's Next Revolution?

A Conversation With Marine Le Pen

Le Pen in Vienna, June 2016.

As the youngest daughter of Jean-Marie Le Pen, the founder of the right-wing French political party the National Front, Marine Le Pen grew up in politics, starting to campaign with her father at 13. Trained as a lawyer, she won her first election in 1998, as a regional councilor, and in 2011, she succeeded her father as party leader. She soon distanced herself from his more extreme positions, and eventually—after he reiterated his claim that the Holocaust was a "detail" of history—she expelled him from its ranks. These days, in the wake of the European migrant crisis, the terrorist attacks in Paris and Nice, and the Brexit vote, Le Pen's nationalist, Euroskeptical, anti-immigrant message is selling well. Recent polls show her as a leading candidate for the presidency in 2017, with respondents preferring her two to one over the Socialist incumbent, François Hollande. Le Pen spoke with Foreign Affairs' deputy managing editor Stuart Reid in Paris in September.

Lire en français (Read in French).

ANTIESTABLISHMENT PARTIES, INCLUDING THE NATIONAL FRONT, ARE GAINING GROUND ACROSS EUROPE. HOW COME?

I believe that all people aspire to be free. For too long, the people of the countries in the European Union, and perhaps Americans as well, have had a sense that political leaders are not defending their interests but defending special interests instead. There is a form of revolt on the part of the people against a system that is no longer serving them but rather serving itself.

ARE THERE COMMON FACTORS BEHIND DONALD TRUMP'S SUCCESS IN THE UNITED STATES AND YOURS HERE IN FRANCE?

Yes. I see particular commonalities in the rise of Donald Trump and Bernie Sanders. Both reject a system that appears to be very selfish, even egocentric, and that has set aside the people's aspirations. I draw a parallel between the two, because they are both success stories. Even though Bernie Sanders didn't win, his emergence wasn't predicted. In many countries, there is this current of being attached to the nation and rejecting untamed globalization, which is seen as a form of totalitarianism. It's being imposed at all costs, a war against everybody for the benefit of a few.

WHEN ASKED RECENTLY WHO YOU SUPPORTED IN THE U.S. ELECTION, YOU SAID, "ANYONE BUT HILLARY." SO DO YOU SUPPORT TRUMP?

I was quite clear: in my view, anyone would be better than Hillary Clinton. I aim to become president of the French Republic, so I am concerned exclusively with the interests of France. I cannot put myself in an American's shoes and determine whether the domestic policies proposed by one or another candidate suit me. What interests me are the consequences of the political choices made by Hillary Clinton or Donald Trump for France's situation, economically and in terms of security.

So I would note that Clinton supports TTIP [the Transatlantic Trade and Investment Partnership]. Trump opposes it. I oppose it as well. I would also note that Clinton is a bringer of war in the world, leaving behind her Iraq, Libya, and Syria. This has had extremely destabilizing consequences for my country in terms of the rise of Islamic fundamentalism and the enormous waves of migration now overwhelming the European Union. Trump wants the United States to return to its natural state. Clinton pushes for the extraterritorial application of American law, which is an unacceptable weapon for people who wish to remain independent. All of this tells me that between Hillary Clinton and Donald Trump, it's Donald Trump's policies that are more favorable to France's interests right now.

Aboard the aircraft carrier Charles de Gaulle, Toulon, France, November 2015.

THE UNEMPLOYMENT RATE IN FRANCE NOW STANDS AT AROUND TEN PERCENT, THE SECOND HIGHEST AMONG THE G-7 MEMBERS. WHAT ARE THE ROOTS OF FRANCE'S ECONOMIC MALAISE, AND WHAT SOLUTIONS DO YOU PROPOSE?

These days, everyone is proposing the National Front's solutions. We recorded a nice ideological victory when I heard [Arnaud] Montebourg [a former economy minister in Hollande's Socialist government] pleading for "made in France," which is one of the major pillars of the National Front.

The unemployment rate is much higher than that because there are a bunch of statistical shenanigans going on—involving internships, early retirement, part-time work—that keep a number of French from being counted in the unemployment statistics.

There are a number of reasons for [the high unemployment]. The first is completely free trade, which puts us in an unfair competition with countries that engage in social and environmental dumping, leaving us with no means of protecting ourselves and our strategic companies, unlike in the United States. And in terms of social dumping, the Posted Workers Directive [an EU directive on the free movement of labor] is bringing low-wage employees to France.

The second is the monetary dumping we suffer. The euro—the fact of not having our own money—puts us in an extremely difficult economic situation. The IMF has just said that the euro was overvalued by six percent in France and undervalued by 15 percent in Germany. That's a gap of 21 percentage points with our main competitor in Europe.

It also has to do with the disappearance of a strategic state. Our very Gaullist state, which supported our industrial champions, has been totally abandoned. France is a country of engineers. It is a country of researchers. But it's true that it is not a country of businesspeople. And so quite often in history, our big industrial champions were able to develop only thanks to the strategic state. In abandoning this, we are depriving ourselves of a very important lever for development.

LET'S TALK ABOUT ABANDONING THE EURO. PRACTICALLY SPEAKING, HOW WOULD YOU DO IT?

What I want is a negotiation. What I want is a concerted exit from the European Union, where all the countries sit around the table and decide to return to the European "currency snake" [a 1970s policy designed to limit exchange-rate variations], which allows each country to adapt its monetary policy to its own economy. That's what I want. I want it to be done gently and in a coordinated manner.

A lot of countries are now realizing that they can't keep living with the euro, because its counterpart is a policy of austerity, which has aggravated the recession in various countries. I refer you to the book that [the economist Joseph] Stiglitz has just written, which makes very clear that this currency is completely maladapted to our economies and is one of the reasons there is so much unemployment in the European Union. So either we get there through negotiation, or we hold a referendum like Britain and decide to regain control of our currency.

DO YOU REALLY THINK A "FREXIT" REFERENDUM IS CONCEIVABLE?

I, at any rate, am conceiving of it. The French people were betrayed in 2005. They said no to the European constitution; politicians on the right and the left imposed it against the wishes of the population. I'm a democrat. I think that it is up to no one else but the French people to decide their future and everything that affects their sovereignty, liberty, and independence.

So yes, I would organize a referendum on this subject. And based on what happened in the negotiations that I would undertake, I would tell the French, "Listen, I obtained what I wanted, and I think we could stay in the European Union," or, "I did not get what I wanted, and I believe there is no other solution but to leave the European Union."

WHAT LESSONS DO YOU TAKE FROM THE SUCCESS OF THE BREXIT CAMPAIGN?

Two major lessons. First, when the people want something, nothing is impossible. And second, we were lied to. They told us that Brexit would be a catastrophe, that the stock markets would crash, that the economy was going to grind to a halt, that unemployment would skyrocket. The reality is that none of that happened. Today, the banks are coming to us pitifully and saying, "Ah, we were wrong." No, you lied to us. You lied in order to influence the vote. But the people are coming to know your methods, which consist of terrorizing them when they have a choice to make. The British people made a great show of maturity with this vote.

DO YOU WORRY THAT FRANCE WILL FIND ITSELF ECONOMICALLY ISOLATED IF IT LEAVES THE EUROZONE?

Those were the exact criticisms made against General de Gaulle in 1966 when he wanted to withdraw from NATO's integrated command. Freedom is not isolation. Independence is not isolation. And what strikes me is that France has always been much more powerful being France on its own than being a province of the European Union. I want to rediscover that strength.

MANY CREDIT THE EUROPEAN UNION FOR PRESERVING THE PEACE SINCE WORLD WAR II. WHY ARE THEY WRONG?

Because it's not the European Union that has kept the peace; it's the peace that has made the European Union possible. This argument has been rehashed repeatedly, and it makes no sense. Regardless, the peace hasn't been perfect in the European Union, with Kosovo and Ukraine at its doorstep. It's not so simple.

In fact, the European Union has progressively transformed itself into a sort of European Soviet Union that decides everything, that imposes its views, that shuts down the democratic process. You only have to hear [European Commission President Jean-Claude] Juncker, who said, "There can be no democratic choice against European treaties." That formulation says everything. We didn't fight to become a free and independent people during World War I and World War II so that we could no longer be free today just because some of our leaders made that decision for us.

PHILIPPE WOJAZER / REUTERS

German Chancellor Angela Merkel and

French President
Francois Hollande in Evian, France, September 2016.

WHAT DO YOU MAKE OF GERMANY'S LEADERSHIP IN RECENT YEARS?

It was written into the creation of the euro. In reality, the euro is a currency created by Germany, for Germany. It's a suit that fits only Germany. Gradually, [Chancellor Angela] Merkel sensed that she was the leader of the European Union. She imposed her views. She imposed them in economic matters, but she also imposed them by agreeing to welcome one million migrants to Germany, knowing very well that Germany would sort them out. It would keep the best and let the rest go to other countries in the European Union. There are no longer any internal borders between our countries, which is absolutely unacceptable. The model imposed by Merkel surely works for Germans, but it is killing Germany's neighbors. I am the anti-Merkel.

WHAT DO YOU THINK OF THE STATE OF RELATIONS BETWEEN FRANCE AND THE UNITED STATES, AND WHAT SHOULD THEY BE?

Today, French leaders submit so easily to the demands of Merkel and Obama. France has forgotten to defend its interests, including its commercial and industrial ones, in the face of American demands. I am for independence. I am for a France that remains equidistant between the two great powers, Russia and the United States, being neither submissive nor hostile. I want us to once again become a leader for the nonaligned countries, as was said during the de Gaulle era. We have the right to defend our interests, just as the United States has the right to defend its interests, Germany has the right to defend its interests, and Russia has the right to defend its interests.

WHY DO YOU THINK FRANCE SHOULD GET CLOSER TO <u>RUSSIA UNDER PRESIDENT VLADIMIR PUTIN</u>?

First of all, because Russia is a European country. France and Russia also have a shared history and a strong cultural affinity. And strategically, there is no reason not to deepen relations with Russia. The only reason we don't is because the Americans forbid it. That conflicts with my desire for independence. What's more, I think the United States is making a mistake by re-creating a kind of cold war with Russia, because it's pushing Russia into the arms of China. And objectively, an ultrapowerful association between China and Russia wouldn't be advantageous for either the United States or the world.

IN THE LATEST POLLS, THE NATIONAL FRONT IS PROJECTED TO MAKE IT TO THE RUNOFF OF THE PRESIDENTIAL ELECTION. IN THE PAST, NOTABLY IN 2002, THE OTHER PARTIES UNITED TO BLOCK THE NATIONAL FRONT IN THE SECOND ROUND. WOULD YOU BE READY TO FORM ALLIANCES, AND IF SO, WITH WHOM?

It's not up to me to decide that. This presidential election will be about a big choice: Do we defend our civilization, or do we abandon it? So I think there are people from the entire political spectrum, from the right and the left, who agree with me and who could join us.

THE NATIONAL FRONT THAT YOU ARE LEADING HAS CHANGED A GREAT DEAL FROM THE PARTY YOUR FATHER LED. AT WHAT POINT IN YOUR CAREER DID YOU REALIZE THAT THE NATIONAL FRONT HAD TO DISTANCE ITSELF FROM ITS EXTREMIST IMAGE IF IT WAS GOING TO BE COMPETITIVE?

In the past, the National Front was a protest party. It was an opposition party. Naturally, its rising influence has transformed it into a party of government—that is, into a party that anticipates reaching the highest offices in order to implement its ideas.

It's also true that a political movement is always influenced by its leader's personality. I have not taken the same path as my father. I am not the same age as he is. I do not have the same profile. He is a man; I am a woman. And that means I have imprinted on the party an image that corresponds more with who I am than with who he was.

At a mosque in Paris, January 2015.

HOW CAN FRANCE PROTECT ITSELF FROM TERRORIST ATTACKS LIKE THE ONE IN NICE IN JULY?

So far, it has done absolutely nothing. It has to stop the arrival of migrants, whom we know terrorists infiltrate. It has to put an end to birthright citizenship, the automatic acquisition of French nationality with no other criteria that created French like [Amedy] Coulibaly and [Chérif and Saïd] Kouachi [the terrorists behind the Paris attacks of January 2015], who had long histories of delinquency and were hostile toward France. This isn't the case for everyone; I'm not generalizing. But it's a good way to have a surveillance mechanism. We need to revoke citizenship from dual nationals who have any kind of link to terrorist organizations.

We especially need to combat the development of Islamic fundamentalism on our territory. For electoral reasons, French politicians rolled out the red carpet for Islamic fundamentalism, which has developed in mosques and so- called cultural centers financed not only by France but also by countries that support Islamic fundamentalism. We also have to regain the mastery of our borders, because I can't see how we can combat terrorism while having open borders.

YOU HAVE SAID THAT APART FROM ISLAM, "NO OTHER RELIGION CAUSES PROBLEMS." WHY DO YOU THINK THAT THIS IS TRUE?

Because all religions in France are subject to the rules of secularism. Let's be clear, many Muslims have done that. But some within Islam—and of course I'm thinking of the Islamic fundamentalists—cannot accept that, for one simple reason, which is that they consider sharia to be superior to all other laws and norms, including the French constitution. That's unacceptable.

For a century, since the law on secularism was passed, no one has sought to impose religious law by bending the laws of our country. These Islamic fundamentalist groups are seeking to do this. This must be said, because we cannot fight an enemy if we do not name it. We must be intransigent when it comes to respecting our constitution and our laws. And honestly, the French political class has instead acted in the spirit of Canadian-style reasonable accommodation rather than in the spirit of an intransigence that would allow us to protect our civil liberties. We see it in the huge regressions in women's rights taking place today on French soil. In certain areas, women can no longer dress as they wish.

YOU SUPPORT THE BAN ON THE BURKINI. WHY IS IT A PROBLEM?

The problem is that it's not a bathing suit. It's an Islamist uniform. It's one of the many ways in which Islamic fundamentalism flexes its muscles. Once we accept that women are subject to this Islamist uniform, the next step is that we accept the separation of the sexes in swimming pools and other public spaces. And then we'll have to accept different rights for men and women. If you don't see that, then you don't understand the battle we face against Islamic fundamentalism.

BUT DOES THIS MEASURE REALLY HELP INTEGRATE MUSLIMS IN FRANCE?

What is integration? It is to live side by side, each with their own lifestyle, their own code, their own mores, their own language. The French model is assimilation. Individual freedom does not allow one to call into question the major civilizational choices France has made.

In France, we don't believe in the concept of a consenting victim. French criminal law, for example, doesn't allow people to harm themselves on the grounds that they have the right to do so because they are acting on their own. We don't accept that, because it undermines the major choices we have made as a civilization regarding women's equality and the rejection of communitarianism—that is, organized communities that live according to their own rules. That is the Anglo-Saxon model. It is not ours. The Anglo-Saxons have the right to defend their model, but we have the right to defend ours.

DO YOU THINK THAT THE AMERICAN MODEL OF INTEGRATION IS MORE EFFECTIVE THAN THE FRENCH ONE?

I don't have to judge that. That's a problem for Americans. Personally, I don't want that model. That model is a consequence of American history. Communities came from different countries to a virgin land to create a nation made up of people from everywhere. That is not the case for France. France is a very old human and legal creation. Nothing is there by chance. Secularism is how we handled religious conflicts that had plunged our country into a bloodbath.

I don't seek to impose my model on others, but I don't want others to decide that my model is not the right one. I'm often offended when foreign countries condemn the French model. I don't condemn the American model. But I don't want mine condemned. I think that communitarianism sows the seeds of conflict between communities, and I don't want my country to face conflicts between communities. I recognize only individuals. It is individuals who have rights. It is individuals who have free will. It is individuals who assimilate themselves. In no case is it communities.

This interview has been translated from the French, edited, and condensed.

© Foreign Affairs

Populism on the March

Why the West Is in Trouble

Fareed Zakaria

ALEXANDROS AVRAMIDIS / REUTERS

Storming the gates: refugees at the Greek border, February 2016.

Donald Trump's admirers and critics would probably agree on one thing: he is different. One of his chief Republican supporters, Newt Gingrich, describes him as a "unique, extraordinary experience." And of course, in some ways—his celebrity, his flexibility with the facts—Trump is unusual. But in an important sense, he is not: Trump is part of a broad populist upsurge running through the Western world. It can be seen in countries of widely varying circumstances, from prosperous Sweden to crisis-ridden Greece. In most, populism remains an opposition movement, although one that is growing in strength; in others, such as Hungary, it is now the reigning ideology. But almost everywhere, populism has captured the public's attention.

What is populism? It means different things to different groups, but all versions share a suspicion of and hostility toward elites, mainstream politics, and established institutions. Populism sees itself as speaking for the forgotten "ordinary" person and often imagines itself as the voice of genuine patriotism. "The only antidote to decades of ruinous rule by a small handful of elites is a bold infusion of popular will. On every major issue affecting this country, the people are right and the governing elite are wrong," Trump wrote in The Wall Street Journal in April 2016. Norbert Hofer, who ran an "Austria first" presidential campaign in 2016, explained to his opponent—conveniently, a former professor—"You have the haute volée [high society] behind you; I have the people with me."

Historically, populism has come in left- and right-wing variants, and both are flourishing today, from Bernie Sanders to Trump, and from Syriza, the leftist party currently in power in Greece, to the National Front, in France. But today's left- wing populism is neither distinctive nor particularly puzzling. Western countries have long had a far left that critiques mainstream left-wing parties as too market-oriented and accommodating of big business. In the wake of the Cold War, center-left parties moved much closer toward the center—think of Bill Clinton in the United States and Tony Blair in the United Kingdom—thus opening up a gap that could be filled by populists. That gap remained empty, how- ever, until the financial crisis of 2007–8. The subsequent downturn caused households in the United States to lose trillions in wealth and led unemployment in countries such as Greece and Spain to rise to 20 percent and above, where it has remained ever since. It is hardly surprising that following the worst economic crisis since the Great Depression, the populist left experienced a surge of energy.

The new left's agenda is not so different from the old left's. If anything, in many European countries, left-wing populist parties are now closer to the center than they were 30 years ago. Syriza, for example, is not nearly as socialist as was the main Greek socialist party, PASOK, in the 1970s and 1980s. In power, it has implemented market reforms and austerity, an agenda with only slight variations from that of the governing party that preceded it. Were Podemos, Spain's version of Syriza, to come to power—and it gained only about 20 percent of the vote in the country's most recent election—it would probably find itself in a similar position.

Right-wing populist parties, on the other hand, are experiencing a new and striking rise in country after country across Europe. France's National Front is positioned to make the runoff in next year's presidential election. Austria's Freedom Party almost won the presidency this year and still might, since the final round of the election was annulled and rescheduled for December. Not every nation has succumbed to the temptation. Spain, with its recent history of right-wing dictatorship, has shown little appetite for these kinds of parties. But Germany, a country that has grappled with its history of extremism more than any other, now has a right- wing populist party,

Alternative for Germany, growing in strength. And of course, there is Trump. While many Americans believe that Trump is a singular phenomenon, representative of no larger, lasting agenda, accumulating evidence suggests otherwise. The political scientist Justin Gest adapted the basic platform of the far-right British National Party and asked white Americans whether they would support a party dedicated to "stopping mass immigration, providing American jobs to American workers, preserving America's Christian heritage and stopping the threat of Islam." Sixty-five percent of those polled said they would. Trumpism, Gest concluded, would outlast Trump.

Fabrizio Bensch / REUTERS

An anti-immigration protest in Dresden, Germany, October 2015.

WHY THE WEST, AND WHY NOW?

In searching for the sources of the new populism, one should follow Sherlock Holmes' advice and pay attention to the dog that didn't bark. Populism is largely absent in Asia, even in the advanced economies of Japan and South Korea. It is actually in retreat in Latin America, where left-wing populists in Argentina, Bolivia, and Venezuela ran their countries into the ground over the last decade. In Europe, however, not only has there been a steady and strong rise in populism almost everywhere, but it has deeper roots than one might imagine. In an important research paper for Harvard's Kennedy School of Government, Ronald Inglehart and Pippa Norris calculate that since the 1960s, populist parties of the right have doubled their share of the vote in European countries and populists of the left have seen more than a fivefold increase.

By the second decade of this century, the average share of seats for right-wing populist parties had risen to 13.7 percent, and it had risen to 11.5 percent for left-wing ones.

The most striking findings of the paper are about the decline of economics as the pivot of politics. The way politics are thought about today is still shaped by the basic twentieth-century left-right divide. Left-wing parties are associated with increased government spending, a larger welfare state, and regulations on business. Right-wing parties have wanted limited government, fewer safety nets, and more laissez-faire policies. Voting patterns traditionally reinforced this ideological divide, with the working class opting for the left and middle and upper classes for the right. Income was usually the best predictor of a person's political choices.

A convergence in economic policy has contributed to a situation in which the crucial difference between the left and the right is cultural.

Inglehart and Norris point out that this old voting pattern has been waning for decades. "By the 1980s," they write, "class voting had fallen to the lowest levels ever recorded in Britain, France, Sweden and West Germany. . . . In the U.S., it had fallen so low [by the 1990s] that there was virtually no room for further decline." Today, an American's economic status is a bad predictor of his or her voting preferences. His or her views on social issues—say, same-sex marriage—are a much more accurate guide to whether he or she will support Republicans or Democrats. Inglehart and Norris also analyzed party platforms in recent decades and found that since the 1980s, economic issues have become less important. Noneconomic issues—such as those related to gender, race, the environment—have greatly increased in importance.

What can explain this shift, and why is it happening almost entirely in the Western world? Europe and North America include countries with widely varying economic, social, and political conditions. But they face a common challenge—economic stasis. Despite the variety of economic policies they have adopted, all Western countries have seen a drop-off in growth since the 1970s. There have been brief booms, but the secular shift is real, even including the United States. What could account for this decline? In his recent book, The Rise and Fall of Nations, Ruchir Sharma notes that a broad trend like this stagnation must have an equally broad cause. He identifies one factor above all others: demographics. Western countries, from the United States to Poland, Sweden to Greece, have all seen a decline in their fertility rates. The extent varies, but everywhere, families are smaller, fewer workers are entering the labor force, and the ranks of retirees swell by the year. This has a fundamental and negative impact on economic growth.

That slower growth is coupled with challenges that relate to the new global economy. Globalization is now pervasive and entrenched, and the markets of the West are (broadly speaking) the most open in the world. Goods can easily be manufactured in lower-wage economies and shipped to advanced industrial ones. While the effect of increased global trade is positive for economies as a whole, specific sectors get battered, and large swaths of unskilled and semiskilled workers find themselves unemployed or underemployed.

Another trend working its way through the Western world is the information revolution. This is not the place to debate whether new technologies are raising productivity. Suffice it to say, they reinforce the effects of globalization and, in many cases, do more than trade to render certain kinds of jobs obsolete. Take, for example, the new and wondrous technologies pursued by companies such as Google and Uber that are making driverless cars possible. Whatever the other effects of this trend, it cannot be positive for the more than three million Americans who are professional truck drivers. (The most widely held job for an American male today is driving a car, bus, or truck, as The Atlantic's Derek Thompson has noted.)

The final challenge is fiscal. Almost every Western country faces a large fiscal burden. The net debt-to-GDP ratio in the European Union in 2015 was 67 percent. In the United States, it was 81 percent. These numbers are not crippling, but they do place constraints on the ability of governments to act. Debts have to be financed, and as expenditures on the elderly rise through pensions and health care, the debt burden will soar. If one secure path to stronger growth is investment—spending on infrastructure, education, science, and technology—this path is made more difficult by the ever- growing fiscal burdens of an aging population.

These constraints—demographics, globalization, technology, and budgets—mean that policymakers have a limited set of options from which to choose. The sensible solutions to the problems of advanced economies these days are inevitably a series of targeted efforts that will collectively improve things: more investments, better worker retraining, reforms of health care. But this incrementalism produces a deep sense of frustration among many voters who want more dramatic solutions and a bold, decisive leader willing to decree them. In the United States and elsewhere, there is rising support for just such a leader, who would dispense with the checks and balances of liberal democracy.

Greek Prime Minister Alexis Tsipras in Athens, January 2015.

FROM ECONOMICS TO CULTURE

In part because of the broader forces at work in the global economy, there has been a convergence in economic policy around the world in recent decades. In the 1960s, the difference between the left and the right was vast, with the left seeking to nationalize entire industries and the right seeking to get the government out of the economy. When François Mitterrand came to power in France in the early 1980s, for example, he enacted policies that were identifiably socialist, whereas Margaret Thatcher and Ronald Reagan sought to cut taxes, privatize industries and government services, and radically deregulate the private sector.

The end of the Cold War discredited socialism in all forms, and left-wing parties everywhere moved to the center, most successfully under Clinton in the United States and Blair in the United Kingdom. And although politicians on the right continue to make the laissez-faire case today, it is largely theoretical. In power, especially after the global financial crisis, conservatives have accommodated themselves to the mixed economy, as liberals have to the market. The difference between Blair's policies and David Cameron's was real, but in historical perspective, it was rather marginal. Trump's plans for the economy, meanwhile, include massive infrastructure spending, high tariffs, and a new entitlement for working mothers. He has employed the usual rhetoric about slashing regulations and taxes, but what he has actually promised—let alone what he could actually deliver—has been less different from Hillary Clinton's agenda than one might assume. In fact, he has boasted that his infrastructure program would be twice as large as hers.

This convergence in economic policy has contributed to a situation in which the crucial difference between the left and the right today is cultural. Despite what one sometimes hears, most analyses of voters for Brexit, Trump, or populist candidates across Europe find that economic factors (such as rising inequality or the effects of trade) are not the most powerful drivers of their support. Cultural values are. The shift began, as Inglehart and Norris note, in the 1970s, when young people embraced a postmaterialist politics centered on self-expression and issues related to gender, race, and the environment. They challenged authority and established institutions and norms, and they were largely successful in introducing new ideas and recasting politics and society. But they also produced a counterreaction. The older generation, particularly men, was traumatized by what it saw as an assault on the civilization and values it cherished and had grown up with. These people began to vote for parties and candidates that they believed would, above all, hold at bay these forces of cultural and social change.

In Europe, that led to the rise of new parties. In the United States, it meant that Republicans began to vote more on the basis of these cultural issues than on economic ones. The Republican Party had lived uneasily as a coalition of disparate groups for decades, finding a fusion between cultural and economic conservatives and foreign policy hawks. But then, the Democrats under Clinton moved to the center, bringing many professionals and white-collar workers into the party's fold. Working-class whites, on the other hand, found themselves increasingly alienated by the cosmopolitan Democrats and more comfortable with a Republican Party that promised to reflect their values on "the three Gs"—guns, God, and gays. In President Barack Obama's first term, a new movement, the Tea Party, bubbled up on the right, seemingly as a reaction to the government's rescue efforts in response to the financial crisis. A comprehensive study by Theda Skocpol and Vanessa Williamson, however, based on hundreds of interviews with Tea Party followers, concluded that their core motivations were not economic but cultural. As the virulent hostility to Obama has shown, race also plays a role in this cultural reaction.

For a few more years, the conservative establishment in Washington remained focused on economics, not least because its most important financial supporters tended toward libertarianism. But behind the scenes, the gap between it and the party's base was growing, and Trump's success has brought that division into the open. Trump's political genius was to realize that many Republican voters were unmoved by the standard party gospel of free trade, low taxes, deregulation, and entitlement reform but would respond well to a different appeal based on cultural fears and nationalist sentiment.

NATION VS. MIGRATION

Unsurprisingly, the initial and most important issue Trump exploited was immigration. On many other social issues, such as gay rights, even right-wing populists are divided and recognize that the tide is against them. Few conservative politicians today argue for the recriminalization of homosexuality, for instance. But immigration is an explosive issue on which populists are united among themselves and opposed to their elite antagonists.

There is a reality behind the rhetoric, for we are indeed living in an age of mass migration. The world has been transformed by the globalization of goods, services, and information, all of which have produced their share of pain and rejection. But we are now witnessing the globalization of people, and public reaction to that is stronger, more visceral, and more emotional. Western populations have come to understand and accept the influx of foreign goods, ideas, art, and cuisine, but they are far less willing to understand and accept the influx of foreigners themselves—and today there are many of those to notice.

Immigration is the final frontier of globalization.

For the vast majority of human history, people lived, traveled, worked, and died within a few miles of their birthplace. In recent decades, however, Western societies have seen large influxes of people from different lands and alien cultures. In 2015, there were around 250 million international migrants and 65 million forcibly displaced people worldwide. Europe has received the largest share, 76 million immigrants, and it is the continent with the greatest anxiety. That anxiety is proving a better guide to voters' choices than issues such as inequality or slow growth. As a counterexample, consider Japan. The country has had 25 years of sluggish growth and is aging even faster than others, but it doesn't have many immigrants—and in part as a result, it has not caught the populist fever.

Levels of public anxiety are not directly related to the total number of immigrants in a country or even to the concentration of immigrants in different areas, and polls show some surprising findings. The French, for example, are relatively less concerned about the link between refugees and terrorism than other Europeans are, and negative attitudes toward Muslims have fallen substantially in Germany over the past decade. Still, there does seem to be a correlation between public fears and the pace of immigration. This suggests that the crucial element in the mix is politics: countries where mainstream politicians have failed to heed or address citizens' concerns have seen rising populism driven by political entrepreneurs fanning fear and latent prejudice.

Those countries that have managed immigration and integration better, in contrast, with leadership that is engaged, confident, and practical, have not seen a rise in populist anger. Canada is the role model in this regard, with large numbers of immigrants and a fair number of refugees and yet little backlash.

To be sure, populists have often distorted or even invented facts in order to make their case. In the United States, for example, net immigration from Mexico has been negative for several years. Instead of the illegal immigrant problem growing, in other words, it is actually shrinking. Brexit advocates, similarly, used many misleading or outright false statistics to scare the public. Yet it would be wrong to dismiss the problem as one simply concocted by demagogues (as opposed to merely exploited by them). The number of immigrants entering many European countries is historically high. In the United States, the proportion of Americans who were foreign-born increased from less than five percent in 1970 to almost 14 percent today. And the problem of illegal immigration to the United States remains real, even though it has slowed recently. In many countries, the systems designed to manage immigration and provide services for integrating immigrants have broken down. And yet all too often, governments have refused to fix them, whether because powerful economic interests benefit from cheap labor or because officials fear appearing uncaring or xenophobic.

Immigration is the final frontier of globalization. It is the most intrusive and disruptive because as a result of it, people are dealing not with objects or abstractions; instead, they come face-to-face with other human beings, ones who look, sound, and feel different. And this can give rise to fear, racism, and xenophobia. But not all the reaction is noxious. It must be recognized that the pace of change can move too fast for society to digest. The ideas of disruption and creative destruction have been celebrated so much that it is easy to forget that they look very different to the people being disrupted.

Western societies will have to focus directly on the dangers of too rapid cultural change. That might involve some limits on the rate of immigration and on the kinds of immigrants who are permitted to enter. It should involve much greater efforts and resources devoted to integration and assimilation, as well as better safety nets. Most Western countries need much stronger retraining programs for displaced workers, ones more on the scale of the GI Bill: easily available to all, with government, the private sector, and educational institutions all participating. More effort also needs to be devoted to highlighting the realities of immigration, so that the public is dealing with facts and not phobias. But in the end, there is no substitute for enlightened leadership, the kind that, instead of pandering to people's worst instincts, appeals to their better angels.

Eventually, we will cross this frontier as well. The most significant divide on the issue of immigration is generational. Young people are the least anxious or fearful of foreigners of any group in society. They understand that they are enriched—economically, socially, culturally—by living in diverse, dynamic countries. They take for granted that they should live in an open and connected world, and that is the future they seek. The challenge for the West is to make sure the road to that future is not so rocky that it causes catastrophe along the way.

FAREED ZAKARIA is the host of *Fareed Zakaria GPS*, on CNN. Some of the ideas in this essay draw on his columns in *The Washington Post*. Follow him on Twitter @ FareedZakaria.

© Foreign Affairs

Populism Is Not Fascism

But It Could Be a Harbinger

Sheri Berman

MIKE SEGAR / REUTERS

Donald Trump at a rally in Lakeland, Florida, October 2016.

As right-wing movements have mounted increasingly strong challenges to political establishments across Europe and North America, many commentators have drawn parallels to the rise of fascism during the 1920s and 1930s. Last year, a French court ruled that opponents of Marine Le Pen, the leader of France's National Front, had the right to call her a "fascist"—a right they have frequently exercised. This May, after Norbert Hofer, the leader of Austria's Freedom Party, nearly won that country's presidential election, The Guardian asked, "How can so many Austrians flirt with this barely disguised fascism?" And in an article that same month about the rise of Donald Trump, the Republican U.S. presidential candidate, the conservative columnist Robert Kagan warned, "This is how fascism comes to America." "Fascist" has served as a generic term of political abuse for many decades, but for the first time in ages, mainstream observers are using it seriously to describe major politicians and parties.

Fascism is associated most closely with Europe between the world wars, when movements bearing this name took power in Italy and Germany and wreaked havoc in many other European countries. Although fascists differed from country to country, they shared a virulent opposition to democracy and liberalism, as well as a deep suspicion of capitalism. They also believed that the nation—often defined in religious or racial terms—represented the most important source of identity for all true citizens. And so they promised a revolution that would replace liberal democracy with a new type of political order devoted to nurturing a unified and purified nation under the guidance of a powerful leader.

Calling Le Pen, Trump, and other right-wing populists "fascists" obscures more than it clarifies.

Although today's right-wing populists share some similarities with the interwar fascists, the differences are more significant. And more important, what today's comparisons often fail to explain is how noxious politicians and parties grow into the type of revolutionary movements capable of fundamentally threatening democracy, as interwar fascism did. In order to understand this process, it is not nearly enough to examine the programs and appeal of right-wing extremist parties, the personalities of their politicians, or the inclinations of their supporters. Instead, one must carefully consider the broader political context. What turned fascists from marginal extremists into rulers of much of Europe was the failure of democratic elites and institutions to deal with the crises facing their societies during the interwar years. Despite real problems, the West today is confronting nowhere near the same type of breakdown it did in the 1930s. So calling Le Pen, Trump, and other right-wing populists "fascists" obscures more than it clarifies.

THE BIRTH OF FASCISM

Like many of today's right-wing movements, fascism originated during a period of intense globalization. In the late nineteenth and early twentieth centuries, capitalism dramatically reshaped Western societies, destroying traditional communities, professions, and cultural norms. This was also a time of immense immigration. Peasants from rural areas, which had been decimated by new agricultural technologies and the inflow of cheap agricultural products, flocked to cities, and the citizens of poorer countries flocked to richer ones in search of better lives.

Then, as now, these changes frightened and angered many people, creating fertile ground for new politicians who claimed to have the answers. Prominent among these politicians were right-wing nationalists, who vowed to protect citizens from the pernicious influence of foreigners and markets. Fascist movements arose in almost all Western countries, from Argentina to Austria and from France to Finland. Fascists became disruptive forces in some countries and influenced policymaking in others, but they did not fundamentally challenge existing political orders before 1914. Their policies and appeal alone, in other words, did not make them truly dangerous or revolutionary. It would take World War I to do that.

That conflict killed, maimed, and traumatized millions of Europeans, and it physically and economically devastated much of the continent. "The lamps are going out all over Europe; we shall not see them lit again in our lifetime,"

British Foreign Secretary Edward Grey remarked at the beginning of the war. And indeed, by the time the war was over, an entire way of life had vanished.

Ain't nothing like the real thing: Mussolini and Hitler in Munich, 1940.

The year 1918 brought an end to the war, but not to the suffering. Europe's continental empires—Austro-Hungarian, German, Ottoman, and Russian—collapsed during or after the conflict, creating a variety of new states that lacked any experience with democracy and featured mixed populations that had little interest in living together. Meanwhile, in many of Europe's older states, such as Germany and Spain, old regimes also collapsed, making way for democratic transitions. But like the new states, most of these countries also lacked experience with popular rule—and thus the habits, norms, and institutions necessary for making it work.

To make matters worse, the end of the war, rather than ushering in a period of peace and reconstruction, brought with it an unending stream of social and economic problems. New democracies struggled to reintegrate millions of soldiers back into society and reconstruct economies that had been distorted and disrupted by the fighting. Austria and Germany had to respond to the humiliation of a lost war and a punitive peace, and both were hit with hyperinflation. Across the continent, lawlessness and violence quickly became endemic as democratic governments lost control of the streets and parts of their territories. Italy suffered through almost two years of factory occupations, peasant land seizures, and armed conflicts between left- and right-wing militias. In Germany, the Weimar Republic faced violent left- and right- wing uprisings, forcing the government to send in troops to recapture cities and regions.

Despite these and other problems, fascists at first remained marginal forces. In Italy, they received almost no votes in the country's first postwar election. And in Germany, Hitler's 1923 Beer Hall Putsch flopped, ending with him and many of his co-conspirators in jail. But as time passed, problems persisted. European economies had trouble getting back on their feet, and street brawls, assassinations, and other forms of social disorder continued to plague many European countries. By the late 1920s, in short, many Europeans' faith in democracy had been badly shaken.

DEMOCRACIES IN CRISIS

Then came the Great Depression. What proved so catastrophic about that event was not the economic suffering it caused—although that was bad enough—but the failure of democratic institutions to respond to it. To understand the difference, compare the fates of Germany and the United States. These two countries were hit the hardest by the Depression, experiencing the highest levels of unemployment, rates of business collapse, and drops in production. But in Germany, the Weimar Republic then fell to the Nazi onslaught, whereas in the United States, democracy survived—despite the appearance of some pseudo-fascist leaders such as the Louisiana politician Huey Long and the radio preacher Father Charles Coughlin. Why the different outcomes?

The answer lies in the two governments' divergent responses to the economic crisis. German leaders did little to ease their society's suffering; in fact, they pursued policies of austerity, which exacerbated the economic downturn in general and the horrifically high rates of unemployment in particular. Strikingly, even the main opposition party, the Social Democrats, sat meekly by, offering little in the way of an attractive alternative program. In the United States, meanwhile, democratic institutions and norms were longer lived and therefore more robust. But also critical to staving off fascism was President Franklin Roosevelt's insistence that the government could and would help its citizens, by laying the foundations of the modern welfare state.

Unfortunately for Europe, too many governments there proved unable or unwilling to respond as actively, and most mainstream political parties offered little in the way of viable alternative plans. By the early 1930s, liberal parties had been discredited across much of the continent; their faith in markets, unwillingness to respond forcefully to capitalism's downsides, and hostility to nationalism struck voters as completely out of synch with interwar realities. With the exception of Scandinavia's, meanwhile, most socialist parties were also flummoxed, telling citizens that their lives would improve only once capitalism had fully collapsed—and that they could do little to help them in the interim. (Socialists were also indifferent or hostile to concerns about national identity and the evisceration of traditional norms—another politically unwise stance during a period of immense social upheaval.) Communists did at least put forth a compelling alternative to the status quo, but their appeal was limited by an almost exclusive focus on the working class and their hostility to nationalism.

The West is simply not facing anything approaching the upheaval of the interwar period.

And so in all too many European countries, it was the fascists who were able to take advantage of the declining faith in democracy that accompanied the Depression. Fascists offered both a strong critique of the reigning order and a powerful alternative to it. They criticized democracy as inefficient, unresponsive, and weak and promised to replace it altogether. The new system would use the state to protect citizens from capitalism's most destructive effects by creating jobs, expanding the welfare state (for "true" citizens only, of course), eliminating supposedly exploitative capitalists (often Jews), and funneling resources instead to businesses that were deemed to serve the national interest. Fascists promised to end the divisions and conflicts that had weakened their nations—often, of course, by ridding them of those viewed as not truly part of them. And they pledged to restore a sense of pride and purpose to societies that had for too long felt battered by forces outside their control. These positions enabled fascism in Germany, Italy, and elsewhere to attract an extremely diverse constituency that cut across classes. Although fascist parties received disproportionately high support from men, the lower-middle class, and former soldiers, they enjoyed a broader base of support than any other type of party in interwar Europe.

Despite all these advantages, the fascists still lacked the strength to take power on their own; they also needed the connivance of traditional conservatives. These conservatives—who sought to preserve the power of the traditional elite and destroy that of the people—lacked mass constituencies of their own and believed they could use the fascists' popularity to achieve their long-term goals. So they worked behind the scenes to maneuver Mussolini and Hitler into office, believing that they could later manipulate or get rid of these men. Little did they know that the fascists were playing the same game. Soon after being appointed chancellor, in 1933, Hitler did away with his erstwhile conservative allies, whom he correctly viewed as a hindrance to his long-planned revolutionary project. Mussolini, who had been appointed prime minister in 1922, took a little longer to completely secure his position—but he, too, eventually pushed aside (or simply killed) many of the traditional conservatives who had helped make him Il Duce in the first place.

Marine Le Pen, leader of the National Front, speaks at a rally in Paris, May 2013.

LESSONS FOR TODAY

So what does all of this say about Le Pen, Trump, and today's other right-wing extremists? They certainly share some similarities with the interwar fascists. Like their predecessors, today's right-wing extremists denounce incumbent democratic leaders as inefficient, unresponsive, and weak. They promise to nurture their nation, protect it from its enemies, and restore a sense of purpose to people who feel battered by forces outside their control. And they pledge to stand up for "the people," who are often defined in religious or racial terms.

But if the similarities are striking, the differences are even more so. Most obvious, today's extremists claim they want not to bury democracy but to improve it. They critique the functioning of contemporary democracy but offer no alternative to it, just vague promises to make government stronger, more efficient, and more responsive.

Current right-wing extremists are thus better characterized as populist rather than fascist, since they claim to speak for everyday men and women against corrupt, debased, and out- of-touch elites and institutions. In other words, they are certainly antiliberal, but they are not antidemocratic. This distinction is not trivial. If today's populists come to power—even the right-wing nationalists among them—the continued existence of democracy will permit their societies to opt for a do-over by later voting them out. Indeed, this may be democracy's greatest strength: it allows countries to recover from their mistakes.

But the more important difference between today's right-wing extremists and yesterday's fascists is the larger context. As great as contemporary problems are, and as angry as many citizens may be, the West is simply not facing anything approaching the upheaval of the interwar period. "The mere existence of privations is not enough to cause an insurrection; if it were, the masses would be always in revolt," Leon Trotsky once wrote, and the same logic applies to the appearance of fascism. In the United States and western Europe, at least, democracy and democratic norms have deep roots, and contemporary governments have proved nowhere near as inept as their predecessors in the 1920s and 1930s. Moreover, democratic procedures and institutions, welfare states, political parties, and robust civil societies continue to provide citizens with myriad ways of voicing their concerns, influencing political outcomes, and getting their needs met.

DAVID W CERNY / REUTERS

Norbert Hofer in Prague, September 2016.

For these reasons, the right-wing extremists in the United States and western Europe today have much more limited options and opportunities than their interwar counterparts did. (On the other hand, in eastern and southern Europe, where democratic norms and institutions are younger and weaker, movements have emerged that resemble traditional fascism much more closely, including Golden Dawn in Greece and Jobbik in Hungary.) As the scholar Theda Skocpol has stressed, revolutionary movements don't create crises; they exploit them. In other words, true revolutionary threats to democracy emerge when democracies themselves create crises ready to be exploited by failing to deal with the challenges they face.

Things can change, of course, and the lack of true fascist movements in the United States and western Europe today is no excuse for complacency. But what the interwar period illustrates is that the West should worry more about the problems afflicting democracy than about right-wing populists themselves. The best way to ensure that the Le Pens and Trumps of the world go down in history as also-rans rather than as real threats is to make democratic institutions, parties, and politicians more responsive to the needs of all citizens. In the United States, for example, rising inequality, stagnating wages, deteriorating communities, congressional gridlock, and the flow of big money to campaigns have played a bigger role in fueling support for Trump than his purported charisma or the supposed authoritarian leanings of his supporters. Tackling those problems would no doubt help prevent the rise of the next Trump.

History also shows that conservatives should be particularly wary of embracing right-wing populists. Mainstream Republicans who make bogus claims about voter fraud, rigged elections, and the questionable patriotism and nationality of President Barack Obama in order to appeal to the extremist fringes are playing an extremely dangerous game, since such rhetoric fans citizens' fear and distrust of their politicians and institutions, thus undermining their faith in democracy itself. And just like their interwar counterparts, these conservatives are also likely enhancing the appeal of politicians who have little loyalty to the conservatives' own policies, constituencies, or institutions.

Right-wing populism—indeed, populism of any kind—is a symptom of democracy in trouble; fascism and other revolutionary movements are the consequence of democracy in crisis. But if governments do not do more to address the many social and economic problems the United States and Europe currently face, if mainstream politicians and parties don't do a better job reaching out to all citizens, and if conservatives continue to fan fear and turn a blind eye to extremism, then the West could quickly find itself moving from the former to the latter.

SHERI BERMAN is Professor of Political Science at Barnard College, Columbia University.

Wealthier World, Poorer Nation

The Problem With the Rise of the Rest

Jack Goldstone

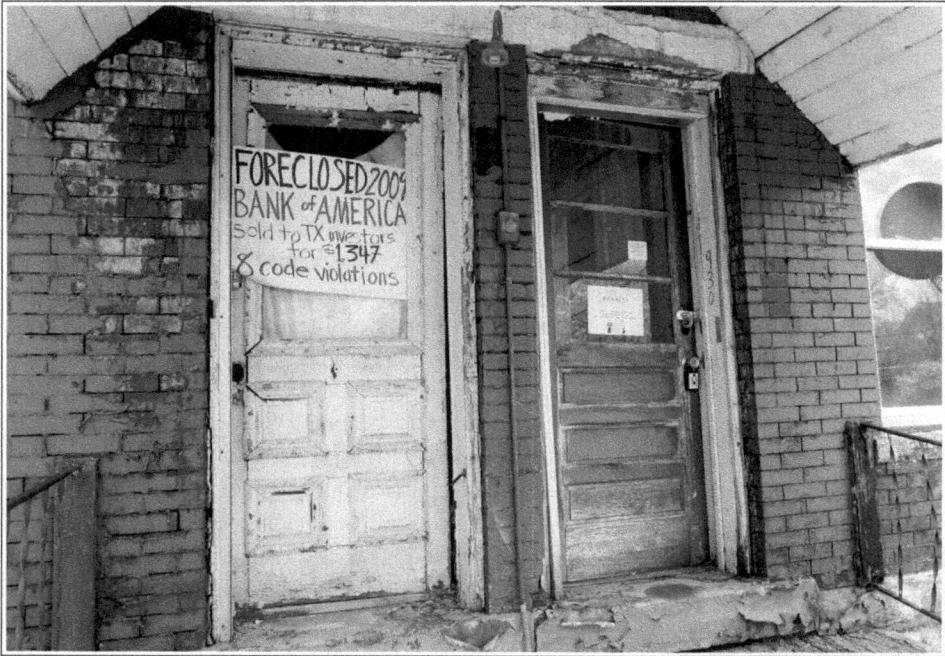

Foreclosure signs by Occupy Cincinnati hang from doors in the East Price Hill neighborhood during a protest march in Cincinnati, Ohio, March 24, 2012.

Occupy Wall Street, "We Are the 99 Percent," and the Spanish anti-austerity movement 15-M may lie at the opposite end of the political spectrum from populist movements such as the Tea Party, the National Front in France, and Pegida in Germany, but they share a root origin: an anger at others whom they feel profit at their expense. On the left, this anger is directed at the ultrarich who have gotten richer—living in a world of $50 million homes, $10 million weddings, and $10,000-per-night vacations—as the rest of the country stagnates or gets poorer. According to the U.S. Census, median family incomes have barely risen over the last 20 years. On the right, the anger is aimed at immigrants who seem to be outcompeting or undermining native workers and threatening their culture and way of life.

And yet the world as a whole is better off than ever before: people everywhere are, on average, living longer lives, staying in school longer, becoming more productive, and, thanks to the Internet, enjoying inexpensive and nearly unlimited access to information and entertainment. Why, then, is there so much populist rage when things have, in many measurable ways, never been better?

Part of the answer lies in the way in which global patterns of inequality have changed in the last 30 years. In the 1980s, the world was to a large degree divided into "developed" or rich countries and "undeveloped" or poor ones. The rich countries included Japan and those in Europe and North America. In comparison, the rest of the world was mostly quite poor. In fact, the World Bank economists Christoph Lakner and Branko Milanovic found that in 1988, average incomes in developed countries were 20 to 30 times higher than the average in poorer countries.

At the same time, inequality within the wealthier countries had undergone a sharp decline, creating remarkably egalitarian societies. From the end of World War II in 1945 to the end of the Vietnam War in 1975, vigorous industrial growth in the developed world generated well-paid jobs for vast numbers of moderately skilled manual workers and midlevel managers. This growth was driven by expanding manufacturing, construction, and professional services—in education, banking, health care, transportation, and retailing—which provided solid middle-class jobs. As the middle class grew, its share of national income rose. In Canada, the United States, and the United Kingdom, the share of national income going to the top one percent of earners went from 10 to 16 percent before World War II to seven to eight percent in the late 1970s. In continental Europe and Japan, which had strong pro-labor policies, the share going to the top one percent fell even more dramatically, from 11 to 18 percent before World War II to four to nine percent by the early 1980s. As measured by the Gini coefficient, inequality based on disposable income (that is, after taxes and government benefits) dropped to levels of 0.2 to 0.3 across Europe and Japan and to 0.34 in the United States. Meanwhile, most people in the poorer countries remained mired in agricultural poverty, falling further behind the richer nations.

Demonstrators on the second anniversary of the 15M movement in Malaga, southern Spain, May 12, 2013.

After this golden age for the middle classes of the developed world, however, the decline of global inequality abruptly reversed course. Since the 1980s, the level of inequality between developed and developing countries has been sharply reduced, while inequality within richer countries has greatly increased.

The 1980s saw the opening up of China, and then of India, to the global economy. This led to a proliferation of global supply chains that produced inexpensive goods and services through cheap Asian labor. There was also a boom in commodities and construction as the developing countries built their own cities, railways, roads, and manufacturing plants. Commodity producers such as Brazil, Indonesia, and South Africa became major global exporters. In addition, the OPEC-led rise in oil prices shifted income from the rich world to oil-producing nations.

In the following decades, wages in the developing world rose rapidly, pulling hundreds of millions out of poverty in China, India, Latin America, the Middle East, and parts of Africa. Many nations became "middle-income countries," not yet rich but no longer mired in poverty, and even the poorest countries (including India and China, which in 1980 were poor indeed) developed a number of fast-growing cities with a substantial middle class.

As a result of these changes, the division between "rich" and "poor" nations became far less marked and indeed began to blur. By 2011, there was no longer the stark division, as in 1988, in average incomes between developed and developing countries. This was a result of the rise of the new "global middle class" in the developing world and the stagnating incomes of the middle classes in the richer nations.

Countries that were once insignificant players in the global economy suddenly emerged as major economic powers, and the former dominance of the Western nations started to fade. In 1980, the United States' economy was more than ten times the size of China's, according to the International Monetary Fund (IMF), even though China was the largest economy in the developing world. Its GDP was only eight percent of that of the United States. By 2014, China's economy was only slightly larger than that of the United States, if adjusted for purchasing power parities. And by 2014, India had also grown remarkably, achieving a GDP that was 40 percent of the United States'. Brazil was at nearly 20 percent.

From a European perspective, the changes within the developing world are even more striking. In 1975, in current international dollars, France's economy was more than twice the size of China's and almost three times that of Brazil. By 2014, China's economy was nearly four times larger than France's, and Brazil's economy was only marginally smaller. These are overwhelming changes, and they happened over barely a generation.

Thus, in the last 40 years the rapid growth of the developing countries has dramatically shrunk inequality between rich and poor countries. A large number of former developing countries have become the top 20 wealthiest in the world: China, India, Brazil, Indonesia, and Mexico, in order of size, all have larger economies than Italy (which is the fourth- largest economy in Europe). Even Egypt, Pakistan, and Thailand now have larger economies than the Netherlands, which up until 1945 was the largest colonial power in Southeast Asia. On a per capita basis, the rich countries remain wealthier, but by far less than before. According to the IMF, when incomes are adjusted for purchasing power parity, the income per capita of countries such as France, Germany, and the United States was 20 to 30 times that of China and India in 1980. By 2014, that gap had shrunk to six to ten times for India and just three to four times for China. The middle classes in today's richest nations are now not that much better off than the middle classes in some developing market nations.

At the same time, the middle classes of the richer nations have also been experiencing sharp increases in inequality within their own societies. The integration of Asian labor and global commodity supply chains into the world economy has shifted wealth upward to the managers of global enterprises. They, along with the financial institutions that provided credit for global investment, trade, and construction, have seen their share of global income leap skyward. In the United States, the share of total income going to the top one percent of earners nearly doubled over the last three decades, from eight percent in 1980 to 18 percent in 2010. In Australia, Canada, Ireland, New Zealand, and the United Kingdom, the share going to the top one percent has similarly increased by anywhere from one and a half to two times since the early 1980s. In Europe, the shares going to the top one percent did not always increase quite as much, rising by a fraction from 1980 levels in Germany and not at all in the Netherlands. In most Scandinavian and southern European countries, however, the share going to the top one percent nearly doubled in the last three decades. But more broadly, inequality is still on the rise. In Germany, for example, even though the gains of the top one percent were constrained, inequality over the entire income distribution still increased: the Gini coefficient for disposable income rose from 0.25 in 1985 to 0.29 in 2011, a greater increase in proportional terms than in the United States, where it rose from 0.34 to 0.39 over the same period of time.

The rise of the Internet, in which trillions of dollars are exchanged and hundreds of billions of dollars of revenue are generated with few or no middle-skilled or manual workers at all, has further shifted the distribution of wealth and income. Thus, Alphabet Inc., owner of Google and the most valuable corporation in the United States today, employs 61,000 workers in the United States; the next most valuable company, Apple, employs 76,000 in country. By contrast, at its peak, General Motors had 618,365 U.S. workers. Even Airbnb with a total of 1,600 employees has a market value of over \$25 billion. It simply is no longer necessary to have a great number of workers making things or performing services to generate billions of dollars in value.

At the same time, the flow of global manufacturing to lower- wage countries has targeted workers in the developed world who once enjoyed high-wage work—within both blue- and white-collar industries—and deprived many of their livelihoods. A study by economists at MIT estimated that 2.4 million U.S. jobs have been lost because of shifts from local production to imports. Thus, for the last 30 years the fruits of global growth within the wealthy countries have been deeply concentrated in the hands of global managers, executives, and financiers. As a result, those in the middle and lower classes—middle managers and owners of small-scale local enterprises, for example—feel left behind and squeezed out of their middle-class status within their own countries. And many literally have been: a new study by the Pew Research Center found that while 61 percent of U.S. adults lived in middle-class households in 1971, by 2014 that portion had fallen to 50 percent.

In developing countries, those who have managed to acquire an education or a bit of capital and moved to the cities have been able to leave bitter poverty behind. Millions have gained white-collar jobs and the appurtenances of middle-class life. Many of those within the middle class now have the means to migrate to developed countries. Although the evidence is strong that immigrants are not taking jobs away from Americans—they tend to take jobs at the higher and lower ends of the spectrum, as physicians and engineers or as construction and agricultural workers—the rise in immigration has contributed to the middle class's view that their world is changing beyond recognition. By blaming immigrants for economic hardships that are actually caused by changes in globalization and technology, nativists feed resentment, using calls for restricted immigration to polarize domestic politics. Even though migration has strengthened the U.S. economy and enriched its culture, the new patterns of global inequality are causing both Americans and Europeans to turn against what should be a source of economic strength and renewal.

BRENDAN MCDERMID / REUTERS

A lone Occupy Wall Street protester sits across the street from the New York Stock Exchange, in New York, June 8, 2012.

The resentment against rising inequality is felt within the developing world as well. Those who remain stuck in the villages and slums, or who labor in mines and other dangerous jobs, feel trapped by poverty and yet are taunted by the spectacle of those who have obtained obscene amounts of wealth. It is no wonder that the Arab Spring, which was very much a symptom of deep economic malaise, happened when it did. Notably, the cry on the streets during the Egyptian revolution of 2011 was, "They wear the latest fashions while we live ten to a room!" In many developing countries, inequality has been rising sharply. In Indonesia and India, the Gini coefficient has increased significantly— in the latter, almost as much as in the United States since 1980. In China, the Gini coefficient has increased by twice as much as in the United States, making China one of the most unequal countries in the world. A recent United Nations report notes that between 1990 and 2010, income inequality in developing countries increased by 11 percent; more important, more than 75 percent of the population in developing societies are living in places where inequality is greater today than in 1990.

This frustration resonates at a global level, too. The large, emerging economies in Asia, Latin America, and the Middle East are angry that they continue to remain left out of leadership roles in major institutions of global governance crafted by developed countries. The IMF, the World Bank, and the UN Security Council are still primarily exclusive Euro-American clubs. This trend is pushing developing countries to exhibit more aggressive behaviors. It spurred China, for example, to create its own Asian Infrastructure Investment Bank as an alternative to the World Bank. That is also partly why China has begun to assert itself militarily in the South China Sea. It wants to prove that it, too, is a dominant global player.

Sadly, it would be unrealistic to present simple or easy solutions to this growing imbalance. But nations can start by adopting domestic legislation that provides more opportunities and essential services, as well as basic affordable health care, housing, and social security, to diminish the scope and sting of inequality within their own societies. In the United States, this involves making college more affordable for middle- and working-class students; reducing the costs of health care; refitting federal lenders to provide support for creditworthy borrowers; and shifting some of the burden of Social Security to high-income earners. This latter tactic can make the economy seem less unfair without having to raise government spending. Income inequality itself is not harmful if the only difference it makes is the type of car or artwork or holiday someone can afford. But income inequality breeds anger, anxiety, and distrust when it affects whether people can educate their children, get decent housing, afford health care, and qualify for well-paid jobs.

Globally, the diminishing inequality among nations cannot be reversed, and this is a good thing. But accepting it calls for a wholesale revision of global governance institutions (including better institutions to cope with the inevitably swelling flows of migrants and refugees). If we do not recognize these changes and respond accordingly, both domestically and globally, the world's internal politics and international relations will become ever more extremist and dangerous.

JACK GOLDSTONE is the Elman Family Professor of Public Policy and Director of the Institute for Public Policy at the Hong Kong University of Science and Technology. He is also a Global Fellow of the Woodrow Wilson International Center for Scholars.

Lone Wolves No More

How ISIS' European Cells Really Operate

Jytte Klausen and Alexandra Johnson

A Belgian soldier stands guard on a road leading to Zaventem airport after the attacks last week in Brussels, Belgium, March 29, 2016.

The attack in Brussels may have been shocking, but it was hardly surprising that Europe was subject to a coordinated terrorist campaign directed by the Islamic State (ISIS). As European officials reported in the days after the strike, ISIS had previously dispatched "at least 400 fighters to target Europe." These terrorists, mostly of European origin, were instructed to construct "interlocking terror cells," officials say, and were given autonomy to choose their target, timing, and methods. It is likely that the March bloodshed is not the last that Europe will see from these networks.

By now the pattern is well established. Fighters, after spending some time with ISIS proper in Syria or Iraq, return home to link up with brothers and childhood friends, who may have also made a pilgrimage to the Islamic State, and pals with whom they have forged bonds while learning to kill in Syria. They try to take the tactics of insurgency to the streets of Europe, killing civilians and targeting government installations. If they fail, they move on to the next plot. And if they succeed, they also move on to the next plot.

NETWORKED DANGER

Abdelhamid Abaaoud was the operations manager of the coordinated attacks on cafes, a stadium, and a concert hall in Paris on November 13, 2015. He should have been in prison at that point. In July 2015, he had been convicted and sentenced to 20 years in connection with another foiled plot in the Belgian city of Verviers. Some time between the foiled Verviers plots, in which two suspects died, and the Paris attack, Abaaoud managed to travel back to the Islamic State and then return to Europe later in 2015. From that point, the French government says, he coordinated four out of six foiled attacks targeting France since the spring.

Abaaoud was not the only man to walk away from last fall's carnage in Paris. His old friend from Molenbeek, Salah Abdeslam, walked away, too, and returned to Brussels. Later analysis of Abaaoud's telephone showed that, as the attacks unfolded in Paris on the night of November 13, Abaaoud was in constant touch with two phone numbers in Brussels. Who the contacts were became clear only after the Brussels attacks: they were the men who helped Abdeslam hide for four months in apartments that were rented using fake IDs. His arrest on March 18 set in motion the next chapter in the unfolding terrorist campaign with which Europe is now grappling.

A placard reading "I am alive" is seen among graffti at a street memorial for the victims of bomb attacks in Brussels metro and Brussels international airport of Zaventem, in Brussels Belgium, March 28, 2016.

The intricate network of connections between brothers, school friends, gang members, prison comrades, and an older generation of mentors from the heyday of Abu Musab al- Zarqawi's al Qaeda in Iraq is as confusing as a long-running telenovela. One of the men who blew himself up in the airport in Brussels on Tuesday was iden-tified as the maker of the suicide vests used in both Paris and Brussels. Now known to be Najim Laachraoui, he was previously known as "Soufiane Kayal." Laachraoui was stopped in September at a border crossing between Hungary and Austria. Also in the car were Abdeslam and a man previously known as "Samir Bouzid." They may have been returning to Europe from the Islamic State when they were stopped in Septem-ber. It was "Kayal" and "Bouzid" whom Abaaoud was calling from Paris.

"Bouzid" turned out to be Mohammed Belkaïd, an Algerian who lived in Sweden until April 2014, when he left his Swedish wife to sign up as a suicide bomber with ISIS. He was killed in a March 15th police raid on an apartment that Belkaïd shared with Abdeslam in the Forest district of Brussels. The apartment was rented in the name of one of the brothers responsible for the suicide bombings in Brussels. Dur-ing the raid, authorities also found DNA traces belonging to Bilal Hadfi, one of the bombers who attacked the French stadium in November.

THICK AS THIEVES

After years of worrying about so-called lone wolf terrorism, it turns out that the really dangerous terrorists are thick as thieves. The high concentration of willing suicide bombers and mass killers in one small neighborhood is only understandable if violent extremism is viewed as a social virus that spreads by a process of complex contagion. Becoming a terrorist involves an act of volition—it is not contagious through mere contact. But close interactions among people belonging to different subgroups who embrace the same extremist belief system have a particular kind of contagious effect: they normalize the abnormal. And soon, large numbers are joining the cause.

Recruiting in the ISIS case is a three-step process. First there are the street preachers supplying the ideas. Laachraoui and Abaaoud belonged to a Belgian network led by Khalid Zerkani, a recruiter and street preacher operating out of Molenbeek. Prior to the Brussels attack, Laachraoui was tried in absentia in an ongoing trial in Belgium of 31 defendants accused of fighting for ISIS. All of them belonged to Zerkani's group. Members of the Zerkani network were also linked to the 2015 Verviers plot, a conspiracy to kidnap and execute Belgian police that was coordinated by Abaaoud.

In addition to Zerkani, Abaaoud was involved with another major Belgian preacher, Fouad Belkacem, and his group, Sharia4Belgium. Belkacem and Zerkani are both in prison now. However, these two men—who are, in reality, gang leaders rather than preachers—have helped send at least 125 Belgians to fight alongside ISIS. Already, ISIS has already released videos in English, Flemish, and French taking responsibility for the Brussels attacks. The narrator in the videos is Hicham Chaib, a former gangster who formed Sharia4Belgium and was Belkacem's bodyguard until Belkacem was imprisoned and Chaib went off to Syria. Chaib is a social media star for ISIS; in one particularly memorable Twitter thread, he posed with four decapitated heads.

Second comes the near ubiquitous prison experience following involvement with drugs, gangs, and crime. Abaaoud was known as a regular user of alcohol and marijuana. The Abdeslam brothers were also stoners, and Saleh's brother, Brahim, one of the Paris suicide bombers, was connected to the sale of illegal drugs. Abaaoud and Saleh Abdeslam were both convicted for armed robbery and may have cemented their relationship while in prison. The Bakraoui brothers had rap sheets that caused authorities to overlook the fact that they were also jihadists. Brahim, who blew himself up in the Brussels airport, was jailed for nine years for robbery involving a gun in 2010, and his brother, the Metro bomber, was given five years for carjacking in 2011. Belgium's overcrowded penal system routinely releases convicted terrorists before they have completed their sentences. Other members of the extended Franco-Belgian network fall into this same pattern of pre-radicalization crime, including Mehdi Nemmouche, who served five years in prison for robbery before opening fire on the Jewish Museum in Brussels in 2014.

The third step for the Brussels and Paris attackers was joining ISIS, which most of them did in early 2013. In the caliphate, brutality is a ritual. After the Verviers plot, ISIS released a recruitment video featuring Abaaoud grinning maniacally while driving a truck filled with dead bodies. After the Paris attacks, the group released a video featuring seven of the Paris cell members carrying out mass executions of unidentified victims—17 minutes of decapitations and full headshots. Having taken the lives of others in this gruesome manner, there would have been no way out.

THE NEXT ATTACK

The seriousness of the ISIS threat was driven home two days after the Brussels attacks, when it emerged that Belgian authorities had seized surveillance material from the apartment of a suspect linked to the Paris attack that indicated advanced preparations for an attack on a nuclear power plant on the Belgian-German border. The Bakraoui brothers who killed themselves in suicide attacks in Brussels on March 22 were part of the plot. The two men had been secretly videotaping one of the country's senior nuclear scientists. The discovery that the Belgian security services had been aware of the threat that terrorists may have been trying to acquire material for a "dirty bomb" came on the heels of news that one of the brothers had been caught in December trying to cross into Syria and was returned to Amsterdam by the Turkish authorities. The Dutch released him. This was just one of many intelligence failures that have already been revealed.

YORICK JANSENS / REUTERS

Broken windows of the terminal at Brussels airport are seen during a ceremony following bomb attacks in Brussels in Zaventem, Belgium, March 23, 2016.

On Thursday, for example, French authorities arrested a man, Reda Kriket, who was convicted in absentia in July in connection with the Verviers plot. Kriket is another ISIS returnee and also belonged to the Zerkani network. Explosives were found in the raid and France announced that it had narrowly foiled another attack plot. The intended target is not known. The arrest in Paris set off another dramatic arrest in Brussels at a metro stop in Schaerbeek. Cell phone footage shows the police incapacitating a man who was waiting for the tram by shooting him in the leg. Video then shows a bombproof robot waddling in to pick up his backpack. The Belgian authorities have identified the man in custody only as Abderamane A., but press reports have identified him as Abderahmane Ameroud.

Amaroud was convicted in Belgium in 2005 for helping two Tunisians, also from Belgium, to assassinate Ahmed Shah Massoud, the Afghan opposition leader who was favored by the West. The killing took place the day before the 9/11 attacks and is seen as a favor from al Qaeda leader Osama bin Laden to Mullah Omar, the Taliban leader. In 2007, Ameroud was convicted yet again of terrorist activity, this time in connection with a camp set up in the Fontainebleau woods near Paris to train Frenchmen for battle in Iraq. Amaroud is another example of the inability of the Belgian judicial system to keep dangerous men locked up.

The European security services have failed badly. For now, blame has been heaped on Belgium. Terrorism is a federal responsibility in Belgium's divided state and local authorities are apparently happy to do nothing. The New York Times cited the Molenbeek mayor saying that it was not her responsibility that there were terrorists living in her borough. Belgian ministers have tendered their resignations. A local police chief in the Flemish parts of Belgium north of Brussels had to admit that "a colleague forgot to pass on information" about Abdeslam's whereabouts that might have led to his apprehension in December.

In recent days, arrests have been made in connection with the Brussels attacks and other suspected plots in The Netherlands and Germany, and in Italy a passport forger linked to both the Paris and the Brussels attackers was held when he went to a police station to obtain a residency permit. The playbook for the Belgian response days after the Brussels attacks comes straight from the French response to the Paris attacks, except that Brussels does not have the emergency powers that allowed the French to detain large numbers of subjects and to use house arrests as a means of controlling suspects. Thus, there will surely be another chapter in the unfolding story about intelligence failures. The Belgian judicial system moves slowly. Suspects charged with terrorism crimes are released to the street and expected to turn up for trial weeks, sometimes months later. And there are still mini-Molenbeeks in Gothenburg, Copenhagen, Vilvoorde, Melbourne, Antwerp, and the Paris suburbs—to name just a few.

JYTTE KLAUSEN is the Lawrence A. Wien Professor of International Cooperation at Brandeis University and an Affliate at the Center for European Studies at Harvard University.

ALEXANDRA JOHNSON is Analyst and RA Supervisor at the Western Jihadism Project.

Watching American Democracy in China

Liberals and Conservatives After Trump

Eric X. Li

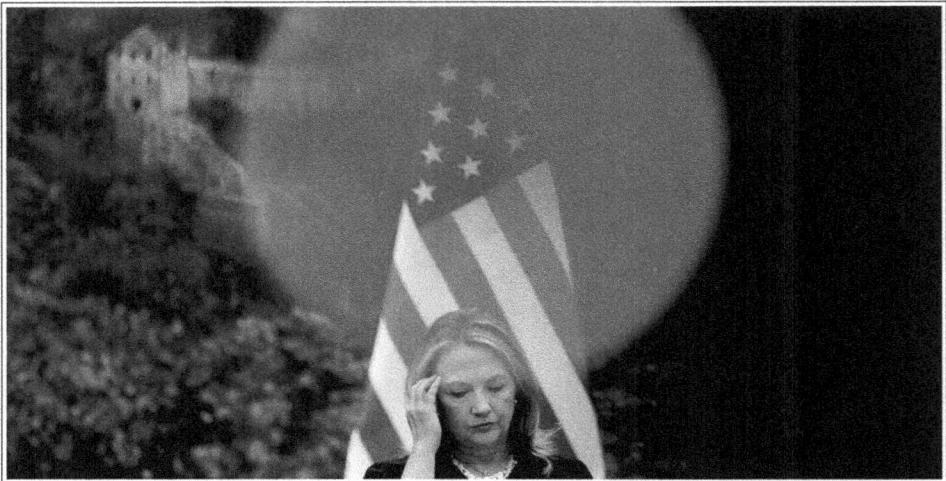

U.S. Secretary of State Hillary Clinton attends a news conference at the Great Hall of the People in Beijing, September 5, 2012.

In this Year of the Monkey, China has been riveted by the U.S. presidential election, and more specifically by Republican contender Donald Trump. Those who usually pontificate on the nature of democracy and about what kind of U.S. president would be better for China are at a loss to explain the Trump phenomenon to the Chinese public.

Two parallel but irreconcilable narratives about U.S. politics have guided Chinese understanding of the United States for decades. The conservatives tell the public that American democracy is a sham in which money and special interests manipulate public opinions and rig the system for their own benefit—the House of Cards version of democracy. The liberals promote it as a system in which the people determine their own fate by electing their leaders, in contrast to one-party rule at home, and as something China must aspire to—the Goddess of Democracy version.

The Chinese perspectives on democracy in general and the country's own future are very much influenced by the divide over the United States, the standard-bearer of democracy of our time. But the American real estate mogul is forcing the Chinese public to reassess its understanding of the U.S. political system. More consequentially, depending on the eventual outcome of the election and its long-term impact, the Trump phenomenon may change how the Chinese think about democracy.

Republican presidential candidate Donald Trump fills his ballot for the New York primary election in the Manhattan borough of New York City, U.S., April 19, 2016.

In the sphere of geopolitics, the experts are even more conflicted. Trump has made China, along with Japan and Mexico, a target of his bellicose language against foreign rivals, which would seem certain to upset Chinese hawks. Yet his expressed admiration for China's accomplishments and his advocacy for restraint in foreign interference complicate the picture.

For those who disparage American democracy, Trump's rise gives the impression that, at least on the Republican side, ordinary Americans are close to checkmating the well- financed elites. Trump is himself a rich man. But that is beside the point. He's running as a protest candidate from outside the system. His policy positions speak to the interests of working-class Americans, and he has so far spent only a fraction of what the other candidates have laid out on campaigning. To a lesser extent, Bernie Sanders' unexpected strength demonstrates a similar phenomenon on the Democratic side.

This is at odds with what China's conservatives preach: it appears from China that the American "people" may thus be able to determine their country's fate after all. One leading conservative paper has had difficulties grappling with the challenge. The Global Times has called Trump "big-mouthed" and "abusive" and editorialized with undisguised schadenfreude that the Trump phenomenon is highlighting the decline of the American political system. Yet, in two other editorials, it explained that labeling the large number of Trump supporters as populists reflected the "loss of rationality" by America's elites and called Trump a smart and adaptive businessman and wished him well.

Students listen to Democratic U.S. presidential candidate Bernie Sanders speak on the campus of Penn State University in State College, Pennsylvania, April 19, 2016.

The official Xinhua News Agency, which reliably paints American democracy as a game for the rich, reported that this time things look different. Trump's wealth, Xinhua said, allows him to buck the system that has been controlled by Wall Street and corporate masters. The conservatives may regain their footing if the Republican Party establishment manages to deny Trump the nomination despite the votes. But at the moment they seem conflicted.

China's liberals are in a bind too. Anger and despair reign. They despise Trump. But they can't quite bring themselves to say that the moneyed elites are right and the people are wrong. Such an admission would not help them make their case for Western-style democracy in China. After all, if the people can be so wrong, how can you give them the vote?

One popular liberal commentator described Trump supporters as forgotten Americans without college degrees and compared them to China's own Maoists. Pundits on Phoenix Television, an outlet on which many liberal pundits appear, either belittle him— for example, calling him te da pao, "Trump the big mouth"—or repeating common charges against him, such as that he is an ill-informed liar. Another liberal commentator called Trump a "naked resemblance of fascism."

The liberals are repulsed by Trump's illiberal outlook. Yet his big electoral wins make them rather tongue-tied, as they have been promoting elections as the only basis for political legitimacy. Indeed, the Trump phenomenon is forcing China to look beyond its two stereotypes of American democracy long served up by the experts. A more complex and realistic picture is emerging.

Confusion and despair aside, most Chinese instinctively understand one central theme of the Trump phenomenon: class struggle. Just about every analysis in China points out the fact that Trump is getting most of his support from the working class. Some pundits are adopting American language to call Trump's rise the revenge of the 99 percent. The official newspaper China Youth Daily ran statistics showing the shrinkage of the American middle class to explain the Trump phenomenon.

This is not surprising given China's Marxist heritage. Since the West won the Cold War, the Chinese have largely bought the idea that Western nations have successfully resolved class struggles through their democratic politics. As the Chinese suffered tremendously from extreme class struggles in their recent history, Western democracy seemed to have reached an enviable position by erasing class lines. But the Trump campaign is showing the world that this may be an illusion. America's working class is angry.

U.S. Republican presidential candidate Ted Cruz speaks on stage during a campaign event in Rochester, New York April 15, 2016.

The Chinese public might be surprised to know that many leading American thinkers have been making exactly this assessment. As David Frum wrote in The Atlantic, just before Trump started bringing in delegates at the ballot box, the current electoral mess is the culmination of decades of elite neglect, and even betrayal, of the interests of middle- and working-class Americans. Globalization, mostly championed by the elites, has benefited the wealthy as ordinary Americans have seen their income stagnate and decline. Multiculturalism, also promoted by the elites, has helped the rich and corporations; immigration has brought lower labor costs and greater abundance of talent while working Americans lost job opportunities and saw their community cohesion threatened by outsiders. One might add that similar sentiments seem to resonate among the Sanders supporters.

As Michael Lind, cofounder of The New America Foundation, wrote in a 2014 essay, "The Coming Realignment," the two political parties in America have long consisted of incoherent coalitions. On the Republican side, capitalist elites coopted many working-class Americans by preaching about social values and identity. The Democrats, on the other hand, also had their own economic elites, who maintained an alliance with ordinary Americans who held liberal social views. In other words, both parties were dominated by the same Wall Street and corporate elites who promoted similar substantive policies that disregarded the economic interests of their own grassroots constituents. In short, the two political parties had absorbed, or repressed, class conflicts within the party structures as a way to remain viable dominant forces at the national level.

Lind predicted that the structure was not sustainable. As social values receded as a main political fault line in American politics, working Americans would unite and fight for their economic interests. This realignment would cut across party lines. Lind was unsure which one of the two parties would become the political base for the newly self-aware working class. In this election, they are represented by Trump and Sanders both. It now seems that, even if Trump eventually loses the election, the trend he set in motion is transforming the Republican Party into the political base of working Americans and is partially dismembering the Democratic Party at the same time. Populism may realign American politics for generations to come.

In this scenario, the Republican Party would become the vanguard of working Americans who want to protect and expand Social Security and Medicare, limit immigration and trade to preserve jobs, and constrain foreign adventures that seem to primarily benefit globalizing elites. The Democratic Party, then, would be the home for urban elites who support, and benefit from, free market economics, free trade, immigration, and interventionist foreign policies.

If this election paves the way for the United States to become a society polarized by class struggle, it would be a teachable moment for the Chinese about the nature of democracy.

The Chinese public would learn that democracy is not a panacea for resolving class struggle. They would also discover that, although moneyed interests have a significant advantage in a Western democracy, once in a while the people are able to take control against the wishes of the elites and influence their country's direction. And, lastly, democracy, practiced in even the most developed country in the world, is just as capable of producing populist and illiberal outcomes as liberal ones.

Trump's impact on Chinese perspectives of U.S. politics goes beyond democracy. The Chinese views of, and preferences for, hawks and doves in American foreign policy may be changed qualitatively. Traditionally, Chinese opinion leaders have preferred moderate internationalists from both parties, such as George H. W. Bush and Bill Clinton, who seemed willing to accommodate a rising China into the existing world order. They have viewed with trepidation Republican neocons and Democratic liberal interventionists, such as some in the George W. Bush administration and Hilary Clinton, who want to aggressively contain China, interfere in its domestic affairs, or both. Even Obama falls into the category. Although the rest of the world may see him as highly restrained in using U.S. power abroad, he is viewed by many Chinese as hostile, due to his pivot to Asia and the resulting tension between the two countries.

Trump is causing a realignment in China. He blames the country for the United States' woes and, as president, would curtail trade that is a major source of China's economic growth. His aggressive rhetoric against China on the campaign trail has been well publicized here. Dai Xu, a People's Liberation Army officer and a nationalistic firebrand on defense issues, called Trump an American Hitler and condemned his victory remarks after the New Hampshire primary as "an imperialist's war-mongering speech."

However, a President Trump would most likely refrain from aggressively challenging China in both geopolitics and domestic issues such as human rights. On several occasions, Trump has actually professed admiration for China's achievements. Both the Trans-Pacific Partnership (TPP) and Obama's pivot, which brought China so much angst, would probably be finished. He has even made statements to the effect that, under him, the United States would curtail its defense commitments to Japan and South Korea unless the latter paid up.

The Chinese have always thought it would be better for both countries if the United States turned to fixing its own seemingly intractable domestic problems. Jin Canrong, an academic and another leading hawk in the Chinese foreign policy establishment, called Trump a pragmatist and said that the Chinese always "preferred to deal with pragmatists." No one doubts that there would be fierce rivalry between China and the United States with Trump at the helm. But China probably does not fear an American competitor. Competition is a good thing. What China has always resisted and resented is an America that seeks to remake the rest of the world in its own image. And that is not something Trump seems ready to do.

In this spring of American discontent, the Chinese narratives on democracy and perspectives on geopolitics are all being shattered. Win or lose, on the other side of the Pacific, the Donald is leaving confusion, conflict, and discovery in his wake.

ERIC LI is a venture capitalist and political scientist in Shanghai.

© Foreign Affairs

The Apocalypse in U.S. Political Thought

Trump Isn't the First—And He Won't be the Last

Alison McQueen

Republican Presidential candidate Donald Trump speaks at a rally at the Nugget Casino Resort in Sparks, Nevada, February 23, 2016.

Presumptive Republican presidential nominee Donald Trump poses as a prophet of doom. "Our country is going to hell," he warns. The United States faces economic collapse, the disintegration of its vital infrastructure, and looming annihilation at the hands of "radical Islamic terrorists." In short, it's the apocalypse: "If we don't get tough, and if we don't get smart, and fast, we're not going to have a country anymore." The time to act is now "because later is too late." If citizens heed his call, he says, there is hope. Trump can lead the United States away from Armageddon and make the nation "great again."

With the promise of a raucous Republican National Convention this week, Americans can expect Trump to double down on catastrophic despair and redemptive hope. Commentators have suggested that Trump's apocalyptic rhetoric marks a stark departure from the tradition of mainstream American political discourse. For example, writing in the Washington Post, opinion blogger Paul Waldman argued that "there may never have been a candidate who sees America as such a dystopic nightmare of gloom and despair." But such observers are wrong.

In fact, many American statesmen have been doomsayers. Some have even used this language for noble ends—to rouse citizens to confront the nation's great crises. What is different about Trump is that he injects his own dangerous brand of megalomania into the country's apocalyptic tradition. Unlike statesmen and even demagogues past, Trump alone offers himself as America's sole savior. Time and again, he tells us that our "problems can all be fixed, but…only by me." Time and again, he promises: "I will never let you down."

It is easy and even comforting to think of apocalyptic rhetoric as marginal and extremist, as beyond the pale of mainstream politics. We imagine a band of vulnerable people who, under the direction of a charismatic leader, have gathered in a rural bunker to pursue their doomsday expectations to a violent end. For instance, the Branch Davidians who were involved in a 51-day armed standoff with the FBI near Waco, Texas, in 1993 were motivated by an ideology of the end times.

More recently, the Islamic State (ISIS) has used extremist readings of Sunni doomsday theology to recruit thousands of followers in its campaign of territorial expansion, violence, subjugation, and enslavement in Iraq and Syria. According to William McCants, an expert on modern jihadism, ISIS leaders and recruits see the wars in the Middle East as the "final battles of the apocalypse," after which the Caliphate will be restored and prophecy fulfilled.

Visions of tribulation and redemption also find their way into the mainstream of American politics. Historically, cataclysmic rhetoric has taken a page from biblical accounts of doomsday. Many of the United States' Puritan settlers saw the religious conflicts in England as the final battles of the end times. To them, England's Anglican clergy were "the excrement of Antichrist." America would become the New Jerusalem prophesied in the Book of Revelation.

On the eve of the Civil War, President Abraham Lincoln likewise cast the looming battle against slavery in apocalyptic terms. Drawing on the biblical imagery of the end of days, he said that it seemed to him "as if God had borne with this thing (slavery) until the very teachers of religion had come to defend it from the Bible to claim for it a divine character and sanction; and now the cup of iniquity is full, and the vials of wrath will be poured out."

Photo taken at the 1912 Republican National Convention held at the Chicago Coliseum, Chicago, Illinois, June 18-22.

Over 70 years later, President Theodore Roosevelt would use the same rich stock of apocalyptic imagery to link his own battle against "special privilege" to Lincoln's resistance to slavery. As the Republican National Committee seemed set to award the party's nomination to William Howard Taft in 1912, Roosevelt gathered his supporters in Chicago the night before the convention. He urged the cheering crowd to fight for a country in peril: "Fearless of the future; unheeding of our individual fates; with unflinching hearts and undimmed eyes; we stand at Armageddon and we battle for the Lord."

Apocalyptic rhetoric has recently been deployed in a more secular guise. President George W. Bush used the familiar tropes of scourge and salvation when he spoke of the terrorist attacks of September 11, 2001, in his second inaugural address. This "day of fire" came after the "years of relative quiet [and] repose" that followed the collapse of communism. The attacks were the terrifying birth pangs of a new world in which different rules of state practice would apply. But, like Trump, Bush also used the language of doomsday to reassure: "the untamed fire of freedom," he said, would reach even the "darkest corners of the world."

Former Vice President Al Gore also used biblical imagery to describe a secular day of reckoning. After showing some particularly devastating images of climate catastrophe in An Inconvenient Truth, he notes that they are "like a nature hike through the book of Revelations [sic]." He concludes his 2009 book Our Choice on a similar note, with a poem that combines references to melting ice caps, ocean acidification, and species extinction with one of the most ominous images of the Christian apocalypse: "Horsemen ready their stirrups."

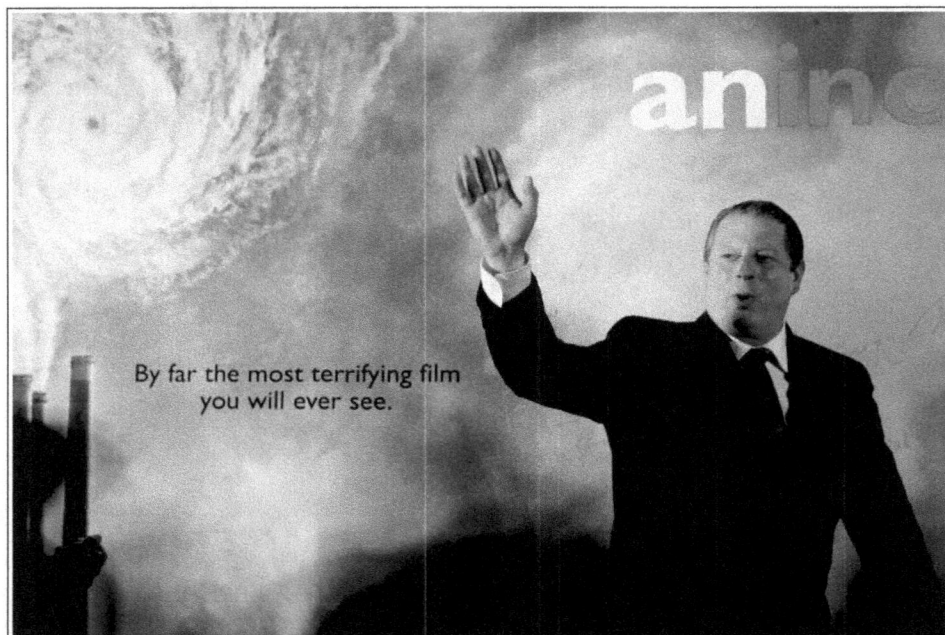

By far the most terrifying film you will ever see.

PAUL YEUNG / REUTERS

Former U.S. Vice President Al Gore waves during the Premiere of the documentary "An Inconvenient Truth," in Hong Kong September 12, 2006.

Why has the rhetoric of doomsday had such an enduring appeal in mainstream U.S. politics? Apocalyptic worldviews impose a cleaner narrative on events that are troubling and hard to understand. For early Christians who heard the biblical Revelation, the trauma of Roman imperial rule suddenly became meaningful. These tribulations were but the prelude to a blessed future for the chosen.

Trump's apocalyptic rhetoric also highlights the confusion that many of his supporters may feel as they contemplate their country's demographic, economic, and national security challenges. We don't "know what is going on," he repeatedly says. But, if he becomes president, we soon will. Today's confusion and discontent become the prelude to an America restored. Like the long tradition of apocalypticism, Trump's rhetoric marries the despair of doomsday with the hope of redemption. It invests the challenges of the present with a cosmic significance. It invites its listeners to see themselves on the edge of a great transformation.

Apocalyptic rhetoric is dangerous for many of the same reasons that it is so appealing. Although its cosmic narrative makes today's crises intelligible, it also reduces their moral complexity. Good is pitted against evil. "Us" against "them." The Book of Revelation promises a New Jerusalem to the chosen, but threatens their enemies with scourge and slaughter. The Puritans drew on this worldview to bind their communities together and to cast out the challengers to theocratic authority as witches and devil-worshippers.

Bush likewise offered a false moral clarity to Americans shortly after 9/11, when he warned the nations of the world: "Either you are with us, or you are with the terrorists." Trump's apocalyptic rhetoric also combines this seductive simplicity with a warning that the choice between destruction and salvation is imminent and its stakes are cosmically high. Later is too late and all means—waterboarding, "taking out" the families of suspected terrorists, and deploying nuclear weapons—are on the table. This is doomsday rhetoric at its very worst. Talk like this has justified unspeakable violence (from the medieval pogroms to the wars of religion).

At its best, the tradition of apocalyptic rhetoric in the United States has sought to unite rather than divide. It has sought to rouse citizens to confront injustices in which they may themselves be implicated—from slavery to environmental catastrophe. It has sought to remind them of their founding values and to give them the moral courage to act on those ideals together. This is patently not what Trump's doomsaying is trying to do. His call divides and excludes. Of those who remain, he demands an enthralled dependence. This is where Trump's rhetoric departs from the best (and even the worst) of the apocalyptic tradition and becomes a kind of narcissistic messianism. Our problems "can all be fixed," he promises. But not by us. "Only by me."

ALISON MCQUEEN is an Assistant Professor of Political Science at Stanford University. She is completing a book entitled *Political Realism in Apocalyptic Times*.

America's Misguided LGBT Policy

How the United States Hurts Those It Tries to Help

Aaron Magid

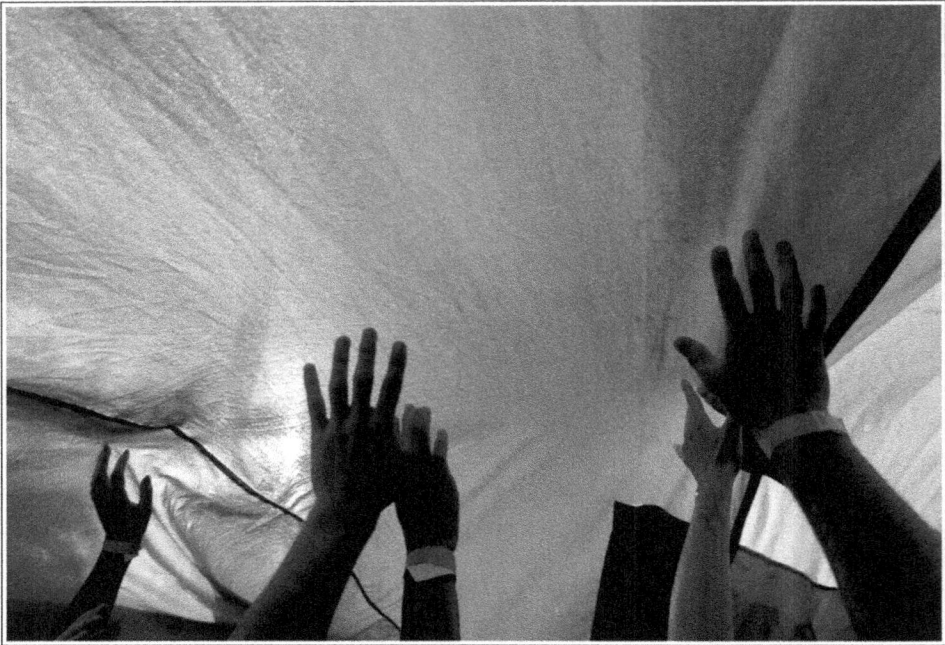

A gay pride in Jerusalem, June 2009.

For decades, the United States has championed human rights abroad as part of its foreign policy. Yet Washington's attempts to balance promoting human rights with realpolitik has often been messy and inconsistent, especially when dealing with rights-violating regimes that remain important geostrategic actors. During her famous 1995 "Human Rights are Women's Rights" speech, First Lady Hillary Clinton riled a key economic partner, China, when she harshly criticized its treatment of women. By contrast, in 1974, Secretary of State Henry Kissinger rebuked the U.S. ambassador to Chile, David Popper, for raising the issue of torture with Chilean officials. Kissinger suggested that Popper "cut out the political science lectures."

Yet it remains an open question to this day as to how aggressively the State Department should promote democratic principles, an act that often infuriates foreign countries or leads to a backlash. Today, the inclusion of LGBT equality in Washington's worldwide human rights-promotion package is highlighting precisely this dilemma.

DOING BAD BY DOING GOOD

Despite its checkered past on gay rights—the State Department expelled gay employees in the 1950s—the United States under President Barack Obama has dramatically changed its policy. In February 2015, the State Department appointed Randy Berry as the first U.S. special envoy for LGBT rights. At the time, Secretary of State John Kerry emphasized the importance of "defending and promoting" the rights of LGBT individuals to American diplomacy. More recently, the U.S. ambassador to Sweden Azita Raji marched in the Stockholm Pride Parade, and in India, the U.S. Embassy lit up its facade in rainbow colors after the June shootings at a gay nightclub in Orlando.

Yet in much of the Arab Middle East, where populations overwhelmingly oppose homosexuality (including 95 percent of Egyptians and 97 percent of Jordanians), LGBT-rights promotion is more complicated. There, widespread hostility to gay rights puts the United States in a difficult position. One might argue that just as Washington has aggressively advocated for women's rights and the welfare of religious minorities across the globe, so too should it consistently and publicly back gay rights, even if that means rebuffing foreign governments. Such a forceful approach, however, contradicts the wishes of many LGBT people actually living in the Arab Middle East.

In 2015, for instance, the U.S. ambassador to Jordan, Alice Wells, attended a small event in Amman organized by members of the local LGBT community. Many Jordanians were outraged, and after her public appearance a number of LGBT individuals were violently harassed, according to a Jordanian blogger who went by the pseudonym Ahmad. One popular local news program devoted an astonishing 70 minutes to bashing Wells, comparing her actions to visiting an Islamic State gathering on the grounds that both would be a violation of Jordan's sovereignty and local laws. Given the tremendous popular backlash, an Amman-based foreign diplomat I interviewed bluntly called the U.S. Ambassador's visit a "dumb move."

Ahmad said that Wells' visit undermined initiatives, such as support groups, that the local LGBT community had been promoting. He explained that, given longstanding stereotypes of homosexuality in Arab culture, the public backing of a U.S. ambassador suggested to many Jordanians that gay rights are part of a "foreign agenda." Ahmad explained that the ambassador stigmatized the local LGBT cause by associating it with the West and spoiled its chance of being regarded as an authentic Jordanian phenomenon.

Given longstanding stereotypes of homosexuality in Arab culture, the public backing of a U.S. ambassador suggested to many Jordanians that gay rights are part of a "foreign agenda."

Ahmad compared the dynamics between the conservative elements of his society and the LGBT community to a high school brawl—just as a student engaged in a fistfight wouldn't want someone else to jump in on his or her behalf, neither does a local activist want the United States to interfere with a campaign. Others echoed this sentiment. When I asked Aisha, another local activist, whether she supports American pro-gay advocacy in Amman, she cautioned, "We don't continually need people to save us." Aisha went on to accuse the United States of hypocrisy for advocating for LGBT rights in the Middle East when black transgender women are repeatedly killed in American cities. When, after the controversy over Alice Wells, five LGBT Jordanians were asked whether they favored additional demonstrations of U.S. support, they all answered with a resounding "No." Mousa, a writer for the pro-gay My.Kali magazine, asked rhetorically: "Is it OK to promote LGBT rights by putting the LGBT community in that country in danger?"

In April, U.S. LGBT policy was again put to the test when the Jordanian government banned the Lebanese rock band Mashrou' Leila—a group known for its provocative lyrics and gay lead singer—from performing in Amman. (The governor of Amman, Khalid Abu Zeid, justified the decision on the grounds that that the group's songs contradicted Muslim religious beliefs.) This time, however, the U.S. embassy did nothing to publicly condemn Jordan's decision—perhaps Wells learned her lesson about the hazards of open U.S. intervention. Although a spokesman for the U.S. embassy declined to comment on the matter, both activists and diplomats in Amman believe that the United States has deliberately avoided gay-rights advocacy in the past year.

Receiving Western funding is also seen as unacceptable in Jordan. The pro-LGBT magazine My.Kali—previously published in English—triggered an outcry in May when its content appeared in Arabic for the first time, leading to false allegations that it had received outside financial support. To maintain its credibility, the publication had to clarify on Facebook that it was not "sponsored by or supported by any foreign governments."

HANDS OFF

For the LGBT community in Jordan, any association with foreigners is tricky. Yet the situation is especially difficult when it comes to the United States. Shadi Hamid, a senior fellow at the Brookings Institute, points to the high levels of anti-Americanism in many Arab countries and the widespread perception in the region that the United States is an imperialistic power, especially after the U.S.-led invasion of Iraq in 2003. Hamid explains that for people "as misunderstood" as the Arab LGBT community, association with the U.S. government can be problematic.

For U.S. diplomats with limited resources, moreover, there are a number of other grave human rights challenges in Jordan that they could address, including the 85,000 Syrian refugees trapped on Jordan's border and the increasing use of the death penalty. And unlike in other Middle Eastern countries, such as Iran, where gays can be put to death for intercourse, homosexuality has been decriminalized in Jordan. Therefore, as one foreign diplomat explained, embassies should focus on issues that can concretely benefit from Western support. Publicly advocating for gay rights in Jordan "won't change anything," at least not for the better.

When it comes to geopolitics, the United States has critical strategic interests in Amman and it should be wary of antagonizing its ally. Jordan has played an important role throughout the war against the Islamic State, such as heavily bombarding ISIS targets inside Syria. Amman also hosts, unofficially, thousands of U.S. military personnel, according to a report from Vice. The Jordanian government is less likely to cooperate with Washington if it feels that the latter's diplomats are insulting and undermining it by publicly raising the issue of LGBT rights.

If the United States truly feels it must take part in LGBT activism in Jordan or other Arab countries that have high levels of homophobia, community members have suggested discrete steps that U.S. diplomats can take. One activist, Nadine, recommended offering emergency relocation and job training for LGBT individuals who may be physically at risk. Neela Ghosal, a senior gay-rights researcher at Human Rights Watch, emphasized that private discussions with foreign governments through, for instance, health and justice ministries, can be a productive way for Washington to reiterate its concerns on the issue.

Finally, Ghosal urged the United States to consult with local LGBT organizations before taking any action, to ensure that whatever it intends to do actually helps civil society. Most importantly, Washington should keep U.S. policy on LGBT rights out of the local media spotlight. (In what may be a sign of progress, both U.S. LGBT Special Envoy Randy Berry and Ambassador to Jordan Alice Wells repeatedly declined to be interviewed about the United States' support for LGBT rights in the Arab world.)

Promoting LGBT rights is a cornerstone of the State Department's human rights agenda. But, in Jordan at least, this promotion has had a damaging effect—delegitimizing the local LGBT community and putting it at even greater risk. Perhaps, when it comes to LGBT rights, Washington should ensure first of all that its policies do no harm.

AARON MAGID is an Amman-based journalist. His articles have appeared in Foreign Affairs, Al-Monitor, and Lebanon's Daily Star. Follow him on Twitter at @AaronMagid.

Debunking Microenergy

The Future Lies With Urbanization

Ted Nordhaus, Shaiyra Devi, and Alex Trembath

Workers walk along wires as they inspect newly-built electricity pylons above crop fields in Chuzhou, Anhui province, China, July 9, 2015.

For over two centuries, rising energy consumption powered by coal, oil, natural gas, hydroelectric power, and nuclear energy—combined with modern agriculture, cities, and governance—has fueled a virtuous cycle of socioeconomic development. It has enabled people in many parts of the world to live longer, healthier, and more prosperous lives. Along with these material gains have come liberalizing social values, the ability to pursue more meaningful work, and environmental progress.

Yet roughly two billion people have still not made the transition to modern fuels and energy systems. These populations remain trapped in what we call "the wood economy." Living in the wood economy means relying on wood, dung, and other basic bioenergy. In this economy, life choices are extremely limited, labor is menial and backbreaking, and poverty is endemic. There is little ability to produce wealth beyond what is necessary to grow enough food to meet minimal nutritional needs.

Although there is broad global agreement that everyone should have access to modern energy, there is no similar clarity about how best to achieve that outcome, how to mitigate climate change and other environmental harm associated with energy development, or even what actually constitutes energy access. Too often, initiatives to address energy poverty have fetishized very low levels of household electricity consumption—a light bulb and cell phone charger, perhaps a fan and a small television—without attending to the broader context that makes higher levels of energy consumption and modern living standards possible. As a result, contemporary efforts to expand access to modern energy have overwhelmingly focused upon the provision of small-scale, off-grid, and decentralized energy technologies that, while checking the box marked energy access, are incapable of serving the variety of energy end uses that are necessary to eliminate energy poverty.

CHRISTIAN HARTMANN / REUTERS

Steam rises at night from the cooling towers of the Electricite de France (EDF) nuclear power station in Dampierre-en-Burly, March 8, 2015.

Energy consumption, not energy access, is the metric that is strongly correlated with positive human development outcomes, and there is a strong bidirectional relationship between rising energy consumption and rising incomes. Modern energy infrastructure has enabled large-scale economic enterprise that creates opportunities for nonagricultural employment, higher labor productivity, and rising incomes. Rising incomes make modern fuels, electricity, and appliances affordable. For this reason, levels of energy consumed within households cannot be disentangled from energy consumed outside the household.

Historically, rising household energy consumption has come as a side benefit of industrialization, urbanization, and agricultural modernization. When most people are tied to low- productivity agricultural labor, there is not sufficient household income to support significantly higher energy consumption, nor is there societal wealth to subsidize it. That is why nations that have achieved universal electrification and access to modern transportation and cooking fuels have, without exception, moved the vast majority of their population off of the farm and into the city.

Rising societal wealth in the urban and industrial core has allowed extension of electrical grids to the periphery, usually with some form of state subsidy. But it is important to attend to the order of developmental milestones. Rural electrification has been the last step toward achieving universal electrification; it comes after most of the rural population has moved to urban and suburban areas, where economies of scale and population density allow electrification to be achieved at lower cost. And even then, rural electrification has proved sustainable only where it is targeted to raise agricultural productivity and hence produces incomes for rural populations consistent with rising consumption of energy.

To succeed, contemporary efforts to address energy poverty in developing nations will have to keep this history in mind. Decentralized renewable and off-grid energy technologies can play an important role in some contexts, particularly where they are targeted to increase agricultural productivity or otherwise support productive economic enterprises and are deployed in ways that augment expanding centralized grid electricity. They cannot, however, substitute for energy and other infrastructure necessary to support industrial-scale economic enterprise. Microfinance, microenterprise, and microenergy are no substitute for industry, infrastructure, and grid electricity.

Off-grid solutions, such as solar microgrids, will make sense in some places. But as a general rule, grid electricity will serve more people at lower costs than any other investment.

The strong relationship between industrialization, agricultural modernization, rising incomes, and energy consumption has important implications. Distributing solar lanterns, clean cookstoves, and low-energy microgrids to poor villagers might make those handing them out feel good. But to end energy poverty, developing countries and multilateral institutions will need to prioritize energy development for productive, large- scale economic enterprises.

There is likewise no pathway to significantly higher levels of energy consumption without moving most people out of subsistence agrarian poverty and into higher-productivity off- farm employment in the formal knowledge, service, and manufacturing economies. Household electrification has, virtually everywhere, been an urban event. And so most countries around the world will need to urbanize to move their populations out of energy poverty, a great transformation that is already taking place at an unprecedented rate. To accelerate this transition, national and international efforts will need to prioritize resources toward cities and their infrastructure.

They will also need to prioritize investments in new energy infrastructure to bring the most energy to the most people. Off-grid solutions, such as solar microgrids and other decentralized technologies, will make sense in some places. But as a general rule, grid electricity will serve more people at lower costs than any other investment. A recent analysis by the Center for Global Development estimated that a $10 billion investment by the Overseas Private Investment Corporation in natural gas generation in Africa would serve three times as many people as the same investment in renewable energy technologies. Further, using geocoded data from western Kenya, UC Berkeley's Catherine Wolfram and her colleagues have shown that many unelectrified homes are within less than 1,000 meters (0.6 mile) of an existing connection but remain off-grid for lack of access to credit and inefficient government connection policies. In short, great progress on increasing energy access and energy consumption might be made at relatively low cost simply by prioritizing connecting to the grid those who already live close to it.

Efforts to end energy poverty are successful when they are pursued not piecemeal but through strategic government industrial and agricultural policy, strong institutions, public utilities, and regulated monopolies. Large-scale electrification has never been achieved without substantial involvement by the public sector, whether through regulation of private energy utilities or the direct provision of energy services through public utilities. Once access to electricity has been achieved by most sectors of society, privatization and deregulation of energy services can sometimes bring greater efficiencies and lower costs. But in the early stages of electrification (and so long as energy consumption is well below modern levels), market-based policies to reform energy services have the potential to impede the growth of energy access and consumption because the profit margins are too low and the return on investment too long when large infrastructure investments are required.

Modern living standards and modern levels of energy consumption and energy service provision simply cannot be achieved in subsistence agrarian economies.

Meanwhile, it is important to remember that energy and electricity are not the same. Most high-profile efforts to address energy poverty focus on electrification. But many important energy services are not electrified, particularly within the transportation and farming sectors. Of all the energy used globally in 2012, only 18.1 percent was consumed in the form of electricity, with less than half of all electricity going to residential use. Another 66 percent of final energy demand is satisfied directly by coal, oil, and natural gas. Most of this is for transportation and industry. Efforts to address energy poverty must therefore include provisions for transportation fuels and infrastructure and for fertilizer production and mechanization of agriculture. The latter are critical to raising on-farm productivity and incomes, freeing up labor to move to higher-productivity urban employment, and creating sufficient agricultural surpluses to feed large urban populations. The former are critical for giving farmers access to markets, providing urban populations with access to food, and, more generally, creating opportunities for economic integration and the growth of the formal economy.

Achieving modern levels of energy consumption for the two billion people who are locked out of the modern energy economy will come with environmental tradeoffs. That is why it has become popular among many environmental nongovernmental organizations to argue for policies that limit the development of energy infrastructure to a narrow set of renewable energy technologies. But faced with a choice of a low-energy renewable future or a high-energy, high-carbon future, the last two decades of global energy development make clear the path that developing economies will choose. The growth of global greenhouse gas emissions has accelerated over that period, as emerging economies have built out a massive new fossil energy infrastructure.

BOBBY YIP / REUTERS

People cross a street in Mong Kok district in Hong Kong, October 4, 2011. Mong Kok has the highest population density in the world, with 130,000 in one square kilometer.

The tradeoffs between ending energy poverty and mitigating climate change, however, are not nearly so zero-sum. Mitigating them will also require a better understanding of the history of energy modernization and its attendant impact upon the environment. Energy modernization has historically been associated with the move toward more efficient, higher-density, lower-carbon fuels and technologies. As such, new fuels, energy technologies, and energy infrastructure should be judged based on what they replace. Where fossil fuels replace wood and dung, as in China and India, they are decarbonizing and positive; where they replace nuclear energy, as in Germany and Japan in recent years, they constitute recarbonization and are negative. What is most important is the direction of travel: always up the energy ladder, toward denser, more efficient, and lower-carbon sources of energy.

In some cases, progress up the energy ladder may "leapfrog" steps along the way, skipping over some high-carbon fuels and technologies. Brazil achieved universal electrification almost entirely through the development of hydroelectric power, skipping over heavy reliance on coal, oil, and gas as fuels in its power system. In Africa, hydropower and natural gas may represent the lowest-cost path to large-scale electrification, allowing modernization and industrialization without heavy reliance on coal. As in the past, the right mix of fossil and zero-carbon energy technologies for any given economy will largely be determined by local endowments, technological and institutional capabilities, geopolitical considerations, and a range of other factors.

Although some steps on the energy ladder can be skipped along the way, key steps in the development process cannot. Modern living standards and modern levels of energy consumption and energy service provision simply cannot be achieved in subsistence agrarian economies. Urbanization, industrialization, and agricultural modernization cannot be bypassed. Energy technologies that cannot support these processes, no matter what their carbon footprint, cannot significantly advance human development and well-being.

Moving up the energy ladder toward lower carbon energy sources can help lower the carbon footprint associated with greater global energy use. However, given current low-carbon options, no practical path to modern levels of energy consumption for all is consistent with limiting global atmospheric concentrations of carbon dioxide to 450 ppm, the level that is believed to be consistent with keeping global warming under two degrees Celsius. Exceeding that target comes with higher risk of catastrophic climate change. But it is important to recognize that stabilizing emissions below 450 ppm is no guarantee that the world will avoid catastrophic impacts, nor does exceeding that threshold assure them. A world of 500 or 550 ppm still brings significantly lower climate risk than 700 ppm. And although stabilizing emissions below 450 ppm has become increasingly implausible, stabilizing at 500 or 550 ppm still remains possible.

For this reason, securing a high-energy, low-carbon future will require continuing innovation toward cheap, clean, and scalable alternatives to fossil fuels. Current-generation zero- carbon technologies cannot rival the low cost, abundance, or versatility of fossil energy. Although there are some important exceptions, economic modernization still for the most part depends on fossil fuels. This is even truer in transportation and industry than in the electric power sector. As such, innovation must take center stage if all the world's inhabitants are to enjoy secure, free, prosperous, and fulfilling lives on an ecologically vibrant planet.

Achieving that future will require pairing efforts to end energy poverty with long-term commitments to energy innovation and deep decarbonization. Climate change represents a profound challenge to human societies. But the effort to mitigate that challenge must not be balanced upon the backs of the poorest people on earth, particularly given that energy development generally increases societal resilience to climatic extremes and natural disasters of all sorts. Lifting everyone on earth out of energy poverty is a moral imperative that we must pursue without qualification.

TED NORDHAUS is Co-Founder and Director of Research at the Breakthrough Institute. SHAIYRA DEVI is an analyst at the Breakthrough Institute. ALEX TREMBATH is Director of Communications at the Breakthrough Institute.

The New Dictators

Why Personalism Rules

Andrea Kendall-Taylor, Erica Frantz, and Joseph Wright

DENIS SINYAKOV / REUTERS

A participant wears a sticker with the word "Obey!" during an opposition protest on Revolution square in central Moscow February 26, 2012.

Strongmen are seemingly everywhere. Russian President Vladimir Putin is omnipresent; the media has obsessed over everything from his latest actions in Syria and Ukraine to his sudden and recurring reshuffling of his inner circle in the Kremlin. Meanwhile, Turkish President Recep Tayyip Erdogan's political purge following a failed military coup has won sustained attention. And even in China, a system that has long emphasized collective leadership, the media have dubbed President Xi Jinping the "Chairman of Everything," reflecting his accumulation of more power than any Chinese leader since Mao Zedong.

It is easy to get swept up in the colorful details of each case. But stepping back, it is clear that these examples paint a much more worrisome picture—highly personalized regimes are coming to the forefront of political systems across the globe. Beyond the best-known examples, leaders everywhere from Bangladesh to Ecuador, Hungary, and Poland seem to be showing a growing penchant toward the concentration of political power at the very top. But is there more to the story than just perception?

It turns out that there is. Data show that personalism is on the rise worldwide. And although the trend has been widespread, it has been most pronounced in authoritarian settings. Data show that personalist dictatorships—or those regimes where power is highly concentrated in the hands of a single individual—have increased notably since the end of the Cold War. In 1988, personalist regimes comprised 23 percent of all dictatorships. Today, 40 percent of all autocracies are ruled by strongmen.

ALY SONG / REUTERS

People look at a building covered in hundreds of posters of Chinese President Xi Jinping in Shanghai, China, March 26, 2016.

It is easy to assume that all dictatorships fit the strongman mold. Vivid anecdotes of infamous and eccentric leaders from Libya's Muammar al-Qaddafi to Zaire's Joseph Mobutu reinforce this perception. But reality is more nuanced. Since the end of World War II, most dictatorships have not been run by strongmen, but by strong political parties, such as the Institutional Revolution Party (PRI) in Mexico, or military juntas, as in much of Latin America in the 1970s and 1980s. Since the end of the Cold War, however, authoritarian politics has evolved, and personalist dictatorships have steadily become the predominate form of authoritarianism.

This is cause for concern because the rise in personalism is creating a number of challenges to U.S. foreign interests. A robust body of political science research shows that personalist dictatorships tend to produce the worst outcomes of any type of political regime: they tend to produce the most risky and aggressive foreign policies; they are the most likely to invest in nuclear weapons; the most likely to fight wars against democracies; and the most likely to initiate interstate conflicts. As the adventurism of Iraq's Saddam Hussein, Uganda's Idi Amin, and North Korea's Kim Jong-un suggests, a lack of accountability often translates into an ability to take risks that other dictatorial systems simply cannot afford.

Russia underscores the link between rising personalism and aggression. Although Putin's actions in Crimea and Syria were designed to advance a number of key Russian goals, it is also likely that Putin's lack of domestic constraints increased the level of risk he was willing to accept in pursuit of those goals. Putin's tight control over the media ensures that the public receives only the official narrative of foreign events. Limited access to outside information makes it difficult for Russians to access unbiased accounts of the goings-on in the rest of the world and gauge Putin's success in the foreign policy arena. Putin's elimination of competing voices within his regime further ensures that he faces minimal accountability for his foreign policy actions.

Politics in China shows many of these same trends. Xi's increasingly aggressive posture in the South China Sea has occurred alongside the rising personalization of the political system. If he further consolidates control and limits accountability—particularly over military and foreign policy bodies—research suggests that he, too, could feel free to further escalate his aggressive rhetoric and actions in the South China Sea.

Not only do personalist dictatorships pursue aggressive foreign policies—they are also often difficult and unpredictable partners. Research underscores that, thanks to limited constraints on decision-making, personalist leaders generally have the latitude to change their minds on a whim, producing volatile and erratic policies. Moreover, personalist leaders—think Putin, Bolivian President Evo Morales, and Venezuelan President Nicolás Maduro—are among those autocrats who are most suspicious of U.S. intentions and who see the creation of an external enemy as an effective means of boosting public support. Anti-U.S. rhetoric, therefore, is most pronounced in personalist settings.

LOUAFI LARBI / REUTERS

Libyan leader Muammar Gaddafi waves from a car in the compound of Bab Al Azizia in Tripoli, after a meeting with a delegation of five African leaders seeking to mediate in Libya's conflict April 10, 2011.

Finally, personalist regimes are the most corrupt and the least likely to democratize. Strongman dictatorships, more so than any other type of government, depend on the distribution of financial incentives to maintain power. As such, these leaders are the most likely to squander foreign aid they receive. The Philippines' Ferdinand Marcos and Mobutu, for example, each stole an estimated $5 billion while in power. Their propensity to dismantle institutions and sideline competent individuals out of fear of threats to their power also bodes poorly for democracy. Instead of transitioning to democracy, the collapse of personalist regimes tends to give way to new dictatorships (as in the Democratic Republic of Congo post-Mobutu) or failed states (as in Somalia since Siad Barre).

Rising global turmoil and insecurity—political forecasts suggest that the world is likely to become increasingly turbulent over the next 10 to 20 years, given increasing levels of violence, economic disparity, and polarization—indicate that the trend toward personalism is likely to persist. Instability could elicit a widespread backlash against the core democratic values of freedom of expression and individual empowerment if a greater share of citizens worldwide comes to see strong leaders as a better option than volatility and chaos. In fact, research suggests that as individual fears of societal change and external threats grow, so too does the preference for strong, decisive leaders who are willing to use force to maintain order.

Personalist rule is not a new phenomenon. If anything, it has been the norm for much of history, ranging from the pharaohs of Egypt to the monarchs of Europe. Although the past century had seen the spread of more collegial forms of dictatorship, personalism has come back with a vengeance since the end of the Cold War. That spells danger for U.S. and Western policymakers. There are no easy solutions to the problems of personalism. But gaining a better understanding of this growing trend and its implications for U.S. foreign policy seems both essential and overdue.

ANDREA KENDALL-TAYLOR is a Deputy National Intelligence Offcer for Russia and Eurasia at the National Intelligence Council. She is also a non-resident senior associate in the Human Rights Initiative at the Center for Strategic and International Studies and Adjunct Professor of Political Science at American University. ERICA FRANTZ is an Assistant Professor at Michigan State University. JOSEPH WRIGHT is an Associate Professor in the Department of Political Science at Pennsylvania State University and previously held the Jeffrey L. and Sharon D. Hyde Early Career Professorship.

A Westphalian Peace for the Middle East

Why an Old Framework Could Work

Michael Axworthy and Patrick Milton

The Ratification of the Treaty of Münster on May 15, 1648 by Gerard ter Borch.

Between 1618 and 1648, central Europe, and the Holy Roman Empire in particular, was devastated by a series of conflicts that were caused by competing visions of political order, great power, and dynastic rivalries, and that were exacerbated by religious differences. This soon came to be called the Thirty Years' War. But the Peace of Westphalia, which successfully ended the German phase of the conflict, has been much misunderstood.

The 1648 settlement is widely thought to have inaugurated a modern system of sovereign independent nation-states in Europe (often referred to as the Westphalian system). And, as the argument goes, when that concept was later applied to the Middle East after the fall of the Ottoman Empire, it actually contributed to much of the region's current dysfunction. But in reality, the Westphalia settlement did something quite different from what has been commonly thought. It set up a system of limited sovereignty for the numerous states of the Holy Roman Empire (formally known as imperial estates, which were the component territories of the empire, ruled by princes or city councils). It also created legal mechanisms for settling disputes and offered mutual guarantees for upholding the treaty's terms, which taken altogether, formed a system of collective security.

Correcting this mischaracterization is not only important for our understanding of modern conflicts in the Middle East, but also for finding ways to end them. Westphalia can be used, not as a blueprint for a new treaty for the region, but rather as a guide and a toolbox of ideas and techniques for negotiating a future peace.

THE REAL WESTPHALIA

The Thirty Years' War began with a rebellion by Protestant nobles in Habsburg Bohemia (the present-day Czech Republic) against the centralizing policies of the Habsburg Emperor Ferdinand II (who reigned from 1619-37), which were disadvantageous for non-Catholics. The war spread from the Habsburg lands and engulfed large parts of Germany after the elector-Palatine (the ruler of a substantial Protestant territorial state and also a feudal subject of the emperor) decided to accept the Bohemian crown, which the rebels had wrested from Ferdinand. Faced with this more serious, larger-scale revolt, which threatened the stability of the empire as a whole, Ferdinand received aid from both Catholic and Protestant German powers like Bavaria and Saxony, as well as from his Spanish Habsburg cousins. His Protestant opponents in the empire, meanwhile, drew support from foreign powers of both confessions: Denmark, Sweden, and Catholic France. These successive foreign interventions prolonged the war and made it much more destructive.

The fundamental problem behind the war was competing visions of constitutional balance, which occurred on two levels: between the prerogatives of the emperor and those of the princes, as well as between the princes (including the Habsburg emperor as an imperial estate) and their respective subject populations within their territories. The question of confessional balance, and of how the divisions caused by the Reformation should be managed and accommodated by the imperial constitution, was intertwined with both of these issues.

The final settlement of Westphalia consisted of three main elements: a reformed imperial constitutional–political system; related to this, a revamped religious settlement for the empire; and an international peace treaty between the Holy Roman Empire and the principal European belligerents, France and Sweden. Although it took five years, the eventual success of the peace negotiations at the Westphalian congress towns of Münster and Osnabrück was due in no small measure to the participation of most imperial estates. An all-inclusive summit of this scale was unprecedented at the time and it was the willingness of the participants to explore unknown diplomatic terrain that helped it succeed. This made it a "universal" congress, and allowed for a settlement that was satisfactory to all members of the empire. The role of informal discussion among the envoys and dignitaries in developing more formal structures, and eventually, treaty provisions, was important to the success of Westphalia. Also vital was the late arrival on the scene of a core grouping of princes from both religions who were prepared to compromise and who acted as informal mediators between the emperor and foreign crowns. Such a cross-confessional party was unprecedented and greatly propelled the peace process forward in its final phase. The participation of the imperial princes to the peace process in 1647–48 resulted in an ultimatum to the emperor Ferdinand III, who reigned from 1637–57, forcing him to reach a settlement or risk losing their support entirely. This intervention occurred at a crucial moment when the congress risked complete collapse as it had become clear that the Spanish–French peace accord, which was also being negotiated, would not be achievable at Münster. (It was only concluded much later, in 1659.) The intervention of this "third party" thus ensured that, although a universal peace accord would be unattainable, peace would be secured in the crucial central European theater of the empire.

The inclusion of the imperial estates in the peace process also shifted the constitutional balance of power between the emperor and the princes in the treaty text. One of the compromises in the treaty involved confirming the princes' "territorial superiority," or political autonomy, as well as their rights to participate in decisions on major imperial policy areas, conclude alliances with other imperial estates and foreign powers, maintain armies, wage war, and make peace. But a crucial caveat was that the princes could not forge alliances (as they had done during the Thirty Years' War) that would be directed against the emperor, the empire, or the peace settlement. The princes remained subjects of the emperor, who retained his power as their feudal and judicial overlord. Similarly, the empire and its supreme courts retained judicial oversight and jurisdiction over the princely territories. The common view that Westphalia created a system of equal, sovereign states that were immune from intervention in their domestic affairs is thus fallacious—all the more so given the treaties' hollowing out of the princes' previously extensive prerogatives in religious affairs, and the right established at Westphalia for external guarantors to intervene in the empire.

The true diplomatic masterstroke of the peace settlement was its adjusted religious constitution, which improved the "juridification" of sectarian conflict—in other words, providing legal rather than military means for resolving disputes. The religious clauses developed a basic framework that had existed in the empire since 1555, which tried to manage religious coexistence legally and politically, while bracketing out contentious and intractable questions of theological truth. The Westphalia treaties did this by extending legal protection to Calvinists as a third recognized confession, and by reducing the authority of the princes over their subjects in religious matters, thereby addressing the concerns of subject populations. After long negotiations and numerical haggling, the parties selected the year 1624 as the "normative year," at which date religious property (churches and endowed monastic land, for example), rights of public worship, and the confessional status of each territory were locked. This meant that the princes could no longer impose their faith on their subjects, and the princes that converted to a different confession could no longer alter the confessional status of their territory. It was an innovative vehicle for the reestablishment of trust between Protestants and Catholics. As Catholic imperial estates outnumbered Protestant ones, it was decided that majority voting would no longer be decisive in representative bodies such as the Reichstag (Imperial Diet) in confessional matters. Instead, the princes' representatives were to separate into religious parties and reach a settlement through direct negotiations. This principle of confessional parity was also applied to the imperial judiciary, with the Protestant members of the two supreme courts being granted a de facto right of veto.

ACHIEVING PEACE

Naturally, the analogy between seventeenth-century Europe and today's Middle East demands an imaginative leap, given the intervening four centuries and the contrasting political, socio–cultural, and economic contexts. Nevertheless, there are remarkable similarities on many basic levels. For a start, there is the length and intensity of conflict, the bewildering complexity of the points of dispute, the role of internal rebellions escalating into wider conflicts, and the involvement of foreign powers. There is also the intensity of religious animosity among the militants, the multipolarity of the international scene, the rivalry of numerous monarchical princely dynasties, and the fusion (and confusion) of religious and political–constitutional matters. Both conflicts have seen the use of smaller proxies by larger powers to fight out their grievances; the exacerbation of more or less paranoid security fears through religious prejudice; and the drawing-in of new powers to the conflict, for fear that their security interests would be damaged if they remained inactive. Both have seen the exploitation of new forms of information technology to exacerbate sectarianism (printing in the seventeenth century and the Internet today) and both have led to a terrible intensity of human suffering. (It is believed that Germany lost up to one-third of its population between 1618 and 1648, and large numbers were displaced as refugees). Although sectarianism was exploited for power–political ends in both contexts, it was also a destabilizing factor in its own right. Before the Thirty Years' War there had been a working compromise between the Catholic and Lutheran princes, but imperial politics became more confrontational and confessional again in the late- sixteenth century. Similarly, sectarian relations in the Middle East between Sunnis and Shiites have deteriorated in the last 30-or-so years, and previous secular-minded forces in regional politics have been pushed out and marginalized.

The main lesson from the European experience is that to achieve peace, an effective settlement must begin with a multilateral conference or congress in which all the primary regional actors come together to negotiate. Participation should be as inclusive as is possible; however, certain disruptive or otherwise unpalatable actors may have to be excluded. Exiles that had rebelled against the Habsburgs were barred from participation at Westphalia, just as the Islamic State (or ISIS) would be today. Participants must be willing to work flexibly and break new diplomatic ground. With the encouragement of the congress, and as part of the process, participants must be prepared, as German Foreign Minister Frank-Walter Steinmeier said in a recent speech in Hamburg, to open up their security interests transparently, and to make some sacrifices and compromises to achieve peace. If the Middle East is not yet ready for this, the experience of the Thirty Years' War suggests that the region will have to endure more bloodshed before it is eventually compelled to adopt the positive and cooperative attitudes needed for forging peace. Herr Steinmeier also suggested that at crucial junctures, the role of a "third party" of smaller powers could be decisive in giving the peace process a crucial push toward completion, as occurred in 1647–48. He noted that the European states might play such a role in the Middle East today. It is worth adding here that the negotiators at Westphalia did not insist on a durable ceasefire before initiating peace talks. The negotiations began and continued as the fighting stilled raged, and were affected by the swinging fortunes of war. Within the Westphalia negotiations it was necessary for the participants to develop a degree of mutual trust, to facilitate greater transparency between them about their security concerns, and foster a sense of shared purpose toward lasting peace. This was not easy then, and would not be easy now—but it is possible. It takes time.

House of Habsburg [purple]; House of Hohenzollern [blue]; the Swedish empire; the Danish monarchy; the British isles; France [red]; Germany; the republic of Poland; the western boundary of Russia.

A central issue today is the Saudi–Iranian rivalry. If the Middle East is to achieve its own Westphalia, representatives from the region's two main adversaries, Saudi Arabia and Iran, must participate actively and constructively in the negotiations. In this vein, it is helpful to study the parallels between the government of Saudi Arabia, given its centrality to Sunnism in the contemporary Middle East, and the Habsburg emperor, who was similarly central to the Holy Roman Empire and the Westphalia settlement. There are a number of points of similarity between the al Saud family and the seventeenth century Habsburgs. The Saudis have struggled with the gap between their position of authority as protectors of the holy places of Mecca and Medina and the fact that they are not caliphs; the Austrian Habsburgs struggled with the gap between their theoretical preeminence as Holy Roman emperors and geopolitical reality. The Habsburgs feared and resented the erosion of the regional supremacy that they had previously enjoyed, as do the Saudis now. For Saudi oil, there was the gold and silver of the Americas, which paid for the military support forwarded to the emperor by his Spanish Habsburg cousins. For Saudi- sponsored Wahhabism and its hatred of Shiism, there was the Catholic Counter-Reformation, that sought to roll back Protestant gains through a narrow Catholic interpretation of imperial law, exemplified by the 1629 Edict of Restitution. The containment (at least) of Saudi Wahhabism will have to be a major part of any future Middle East settlement. But Saudi Arabia will have to be nursed through any such negotiation process, just as the other parties at Westphalia had to cater to the emperor's interests.

SECURING PEACE

Any new settlement in the Middle East must build on traditional religious, legal, and other structures native to the region, just as Westphalia was squarely based on a preexisting but renegotiated imperial system. Imposing a European template is out of the question; the idea is rather to apply the underlying principles and the experience of Westphalia to the Middle East.

The first principle involves limiting the sovereignty of most states or rulers in the region by giving a degree of protection to citizens against their own rulers, and giving subjects or citizens the right to appeal to a higher legal authority. This could be some form of a court, as was the case in the Holy Roman Empire, where litigation became crucial in defusing tensions and preventing conflict.

The Holy Roman Empire's two supreme judicial tribunals were crucial in the defense of Westphalian terms and rights. The courts more often mediated between conflicting princes than doled out verdicts after a trial, but this was a good example where informal conflict resolution mechanisms worked better than formal ones. By including both Catholics and Protestants among its judges, the courts regained a degree of confidence among the various confessions, and many cases were resolved without ever coming to a formal judgement.

By accepting appeals from subjects who could sue their rulers at the courts, the imperial judicial system served as a safety valve against pent-up popular discontent. The courts helped to maintain the status quo, and in particular, the conditional sovereignty that limited imperial princes' power by overseeing and policing their conduct, including their treatment of their subjects. The Middle East has no preexisting supra-statal judicial structure as such, but the United Nations as an institution does have an international courts system and conflict-resolution mechanisms that could be adapted to this purpose. Some states may be reluctant to accept limitations on their sovereignty, but if such limitations were to come with a UN label they may be more palatable, especially as it becomes clear that the only alternative is unending violence.

A second principle is recognizing that peace will only last if external guarantors collectively enforce respect among states for their people's basic rights of religion, property, and due process. One of the key legacies of the Westphalian system was its innovative guarantor system, which enabled the signatories to enforce the terms of the settlement and set up a collective security system that encompassed both the internal guarantors (emperor and princes) and the external guarantors (France and Sweden). The latter integrated this system into the broader international order of early modern Europe.

The guarantee was most salient when the integrity and the constitutional balance of the empire was under threat, which in some cases emanated from one or more of the guarantors themselves—notably from the French monarch, Louis XIV, in the latter part of the seventeenth century. The guarantors that were not party to the dispute would then usually step in and defend the Westphalian order—either out of principled conviction or geopolitical self-interest, or a combination of the two.

Since none of the internal judicial mechanisms could compel the emperor to adhere to imperial law, the external guarantee was a necessary complement; it encouraged restraint on the part of both the emperor and the princes, deterred obvious breaches of the peace agreement and the law, and incentivized respect for the confessional rights and princely prerogatives that were confirmed at Westphalia. The guarantor system also proved able to evolve and grow in response to shifting international currents: Sweden's geopolitical decline over the course of the eighteenth century made it less capable of exercising the guarantee effectively (although in formal terms, it retained its full status until the demise of the empire in 1806), whereas Russia's growing power vaulted it into guarantor status in 1779. A guarantor system for the Middle East would need to be similarly flexible.

Although Louis XIV and other monarchs tried to take advantage of their guarantor status to advance their power or political self-interest, the norms established by Westphalia served as a restraint even when breached. For instance, the question of breach was discussed, including by the king himself, in terms of the Westphalia norms, with an inherent prejudice toward peace. Eventually, Louis XIV's geopolitical adventures ended in failure and the norms of behavior established by Westphalia played an important part in obstructing his ambitions and bringing together other European states in an alliance against him. The success of the guarantor system was due, in part, to a widespread normative acceptance of outside intervention for the protection of rights and liberties. There was also a corresponding, entrenched tradition within the empire of seeking foreign assistance. This, along with the decentralized nature of the empire, helped make the external guarantor system effective.

In order to find appropriate external guarantors for a future Middle Eastern settlement, one would need to establish mechanisms that reflect prevailing power distributions, but that also have regional legitimacy. Some have suggested that the European system in the early modern period had a greater degree of cultural homogeneity than the Middle East has now. In that sense, having Sweden and France serve as guarantors did not seem as "external" as the United States and the European Union, for example, would be to the Middle East today. The United Nations may be the only potential external guarantor with real legitimacy since it includes Middle Eastern representation, but its legitimacy comes at the cost of effectiveness, to some extent.

For an external guarantee system to be effective it needs to be backed up by military force, even if that force is never used. Although the United States and the EU would be reluctant to commit to such an arrangement, regional powers like Saudi Arabia and Iran might be more willing. Turkey might also be willing to take on a greater role. In this context, one must face the risk of guarantor interventions exacerbating existing tensions on the ground, not least for being perceived as guided by self-interest, as was the case of France under Louis XIV. Therefore, it would be desirable when establishing the guarantor system to match the interests of the guarantors with what is needed to maintain the system. For Saudi Arabia, it is important to maintain the regime's position as the preeminent state of Sunni Islam, boosted by its role as the guardian of the holy places of Mecca and Medina. Iran's leaders feel a certain duty to speak for the more or less oppressed Shiite minorities in the region.

A third principle or element derived from Westphalia could be for the Middle East to determine its own "normative year"—to reset the rights of public worship and the intercommunal balance of local states and actors at an equitable, agreed upon date in the past. No subject or citizen could be legally excluded from civic office on the basis of religion. Within each state, there would be a guarantee of at least a minimum level of rights and protections for minority groups. This provision also implies that the established borders between states in the region would be preserved and upheld as part of the settlement, as was the case at Westphalia. Selecting a date for the normative year would be contentious, and it might be more useful to do so in some contexts than others. But applied judiciously and flexibly (in the Westphalia treaties there was some variable geometry on this point, with 1624 being the general normative date, but 1618 used in some special cases) it could be a useful tool in peacemaking. Instead of confessional conflict being eradicated by Westphalia, it was transformed into legal processes—another example of the "juridification" of conflict characteristic of the Holy Roman Empire. Litigation, negotiation, and diplomacy became crucial in defusing tensions and turning hot conflict into diplomatic tension, notably during the German confessional crisis of 1719. This was triggered by the attempts of several Catholic princes in the Rhineland to undermine their Protestant subjects' religious rights. In response, north German Protestant powers threatened armed intervention. Armed conflict was avoided because the involved parties complied with politico–judicial mandates from Vienna to restore the states to their pre-crisis conditions.

It is almost conventional wisdom that the heterogeneity of actors in the Middle East undermines the chances of reaching a general settlement like that of Westphalia. But the Holy Roman Empire also contained a diverse set of actors and interests, traumatically divided by war and atrocity. Even if it is impossible (and perhaps undesirable) to try to transport solutions wholesale as blueprints or templates from region to region, the experience of Westphalia is valuable. It shows, importantly, that peace can always be brokered—regardless of the complexity, duration, and intensity of the conflict—with some help, as the German Foreign Minister Steinmeier has said, from discreet, experienced, and authoritative diplomatic negotiators. And, centuries later, Westphalia shows us how such peace can be found.

MICHAEL AXWORTHY is Senior Lecturer and Director of the Centre for Persian and Iranian Studies at the University of Exeter, United Kingdom. PATRICK MILTON is a Postdoctoral Research Fellow at Free University of Berlin. The ideas in this article are drawn from a project to explore ways in which the Peace of Westphalia can inform peacemaking in the contemporary Middle East. This project was launched by Brendan Simms and ourselves at the beginning of 2016 under the aegis of the Cambridge Forum for Geopolitics, and will be taken forward from this autumn in association with the Koerber Stiftung in Berlin.

A Tale of Two Statues

Putin, Stalin, and Russia's Bloody Past

Alexander Baunov

The statue of Vladimir the Great in Moscow, November 2016.

Russia is preoccupied with two new statues. Both are of medieval monarchs, but the messages they convey are very different. On November 4, a monument to the tenth-century Russian King Vladimir the Great was erected near the Kremlin in a not so subtle tribute to the country's current ruler. Meanwhile, a new equestrian statue of Ivan the Terrible installed in the city of Oryol, southwest of Moscow, is a much less welcome apparition for Russia's current ruler.

The monument to Vladimir, who is known for converting to Christianity and for ruling the territory comprising both modern Ukraine and Russia, honors his namesake and the current proprietor of the Kremlin, Vladimir Putin. Its construction is an obvious act of homage by the elites to their current boss; Putin has floated the idea of Russia as a separate Orthodox civilization, and the statue was erected in front of the Kremlin's Borovitskaya Tower, where Putin and other officials enter the building. By contrast, the monument to Ivan the Terrible is an act of veneration of Stalin by proxy and is in line with plans by local mayors, governors, and Communist Party activists to put up Stalin memorials across Russia—a campaign that is causing the Kremlin quite a headache.

In contemporary Russia, outright approbation of Stalin is still frowned upon. But a memorial to Ivan the Terrible is an indirect and safe way to celebrate the Soviet dictator's still popularly endorsed propensity for sacrificing the top echelons of the ruling class. At the unveiling of the new statue in Oryol, the regional governor, Vadim Potomsky, and the minister of culture, Vladimir Medinsky, put it succinctly if incorrectly: Ivan was a man who killed only a few thousand people—and only members of the elite.

This is the kind of ruler most of the people seem to desire—and it is not the kind of ruler Putin is. Putin represses freethinking, of course, just as Ivan and Stalin did, but he is not interested in bloody purges of the elite. On the contrary, he tends to stubbornly defend unpopular appointees, even though that damages his reputation as a leader. In answer to questions about any given official's suitability for his or her job, Putin repeats the same mantra: If you start to sacrifice your employees, who will be left to work with you in the future?

Putin's loyalty to his subordinates most sharply distinguishes him from the popular idea of the Russian ruler, who is supposed to be kind to ordinary folk but tough on elites, an executioner of generals but a father to the soldiers.

The monument to Ivan the Terrible is an act of veneration of Stalin by proxy

---

Ivan the Terrible was that kind of sovereign. He would not spare even his own son from death—not to mention aristocrats, members of the Federal Assembly, or petty bureaucrats—but he did struggle against external and internal enemies of the Russian Orthodox community, considerably enlarge the country, and execute many corrupt boyar nobles and local rulers that the public held responsible for every ill, from poverty to natural disasters. Of course, the truth is that his reign saw the executions of thousands of ordinary people, too. Stalin himself grasped the genius of Ivan's strategy, and it is no coincidence that he personally oversaw the script of Sergei Eisenstein's film Ivan the Terrible. He is known to have explained to Eisenstein that it was okay to depict repression, but the cause and value of it must be apparent.

If Putin tried to use the figures of Stalin and Ivan the Terrible in the same way, he would be regarded as an impostor. That's why he is far more comfortable with Vladimir the Great. Besides sharing a name, Putin, like Vladimir, who baptized Russia, believes he is saving Russia's Orthodox soul. And like Vladimir, who through the adoption of Christianity introduced medieval Russia into the circle of big European powers, Putin believes he is making Russia great again.

(Left to Right) Natalia Solzhenitsyn (widow of Alexander), Russian President Vladimir Putin, Orthodox Patriach Kirill, and Prime Minister Dmitry Medvedev at the unveiling of the statue to Vladimir the Great, November 2016.

The Russian president is also happy summoning up the memory of Pyotr Stolypin, who served as prime minister of Russia from 1906 to 1911 and was famous for both battling terrorists and implementing reforms. Despite being virtually unknown to the public, Stolypin received more votes than Stalin in televised debates on great Russian historical figures—an outcome that would have been impossible without instructions from above. And in 2012, a statue of Stolypin was put up in Moscow outside the White House, where Putin had recently been working as prime minister.

Like Ivan, Stolypin is remembered for his cruelty, but it was a specific kind of cruelty—condemned at the time by Leo Tolstoy—in which he severely repressed the peasants in his efforts to institute agrarian reform. That is not the kind of cruelty that the Russian public consciousness has ever approved of. Historically, average folk have believed that the leader is good but shielded from the suffering of the people by the corrupt boyars. It is that class that must be dismantled, so that the leader can better rule.

Because the veneration of Ivan and Stalin sits poorly with the Putin regime, it is not surprising that it tried to downplay the new statue. State television did not cover the unveiling of the Ivan the Terrible statue in Oryol with any great enthusiasm. Viewers were shown both joyful residents and unhappy citizens and historians who reminded them of Ivan's bloody deeds, and the news anchors reported on the event as a controversial local initiative.

And controversial it is. Potomsky, who erected the Ivan monument, is a presidential appointee but also a member of the Communist Party of the Russian Federation, which is considered to be (and is) a part of Putin's system but provides a slight challenge to Putin from the left. Proposed Stalin statues in Irkutsk and Novosibirsk are likewise the brainchildren of politicians who are not fully loyal to the Kremlin. In a way, Putin has himself to blame for their jabs.

In the first phase of his presidency, Putin made a clear distinction between economic and ideological life in Russia. Russians mourning the loss of the Soviet Union were encouraged to put up with the unpopular market economy. In return they were compensated with the old beloved melody of the Soviet national anthem, the red flag flying on Victory Day, military parades, and a new historiography that did not reject the Soviet period but incorporated it into an overarching historical narrative.

As economic growth slowed, the number of symbolic concessions handed out by the Kremlin increased. At the same time, however, Putin began to break with Russia's Western-leaning middle class and restructure his elite regime into a populist one, moving the locus of his own support from the political, financial, and intellectual elite to the "common people." Putin started to present himself as a politician close to the people, who bypassed the elite. Yet he had originated as an appointee of the elite, so he is still loyal to them. Outside Russia, Putin still looks powerful in a way that has nothing to do with his country's nuclear arsenal or brazen foreign policy. That is because, despite his political background and a leadership style that is more head of bureaucracy than leader of the people, he has impressed on the world the image of a ruler who communicates with the people and circumvents the elite. In parallel, Russia has started producing anti-elite information output for a foreign audience through media outlets such as RT (formerly Russia Today) and Sputnik.

And yet in comparison with many foreign leaders who have resorted to populism, Putin is still hopelessly elitist. He is the center of the establishment, not the alternative to it. Moreover, his classical conservative authoritarianism steers clear of revolutionary activity and refrains from carrying out purges.

Now Ivan the Terrible has ridden in to remind him that his strategy might not be sustainable. Still, on Russia's Day of National Unity, November 4, the same day the Vladimir monument was inaugurated near the Kremlin, some participants of a pro-government march organized by the authorities in Moscow were chanting, "Purges, purges."

ALEXANDER BAUNOV is a Senior Associate at the Carnegie Moscow Center and Editor in Chief of Carnegie.ru.

Global Trumpism

Why Trump's Victory Was 30 Years in the Making and Why It Won't Stop Here

Mark Blyth

Nigel Farage at Trump Tower, New York, November 2016.

Trump's victory was predictable, and was predicted, but not by looking at polls. Polling has taken a beating recently having failed to predict the victory of David Cameron's Conservative Party in the British general elections, then Brexit, and now the election of Donald Trump. One can argue about what's wrong with the methods involved, but more fundamentally what polls do is to treat these phenomena as isolated events when they are in fact the product of a common set of causes 30 years in the making.

There are two issues at play here. The first is known as Galton's problem, after Sir Francis Galton, the inventor of much of modern statistics. Galton's problem is that when we treat cases as independent—the British election, Brexit, the U.S. election—they may not actually be independent. There may be' links between the cases—think of Brexit's Nigel Farage showing up at Trump's rallies—and there could be subtler contagion or mimicry effects in play as information from one case "infects" the other, changing the dynamics of the system as a whole. Could there then be a higher set of drivers in the global economy pushing the world in a direction where Trump is really just one part of a more global pattern of events?

Consider that there are many Trumpets blowing around the developed world, on both the right and the left. On the one side, insurgent right-wing parties are bulldozing the vote shares of traditional centrist parties all over Europe. For example, the Finns Party is the second-largest party in the Finnish parliament. In Sweden, the Swedish Democrats are the third-largest party in parliament. In Hungary, Prime Minister Viktor Orban's political party, Fidesz, runs the country having won two elections. Meanwhile in France, the most popular political party is the National Front, which in all scenarios but one—whatever such exercises are actually worth—is expected to win the first round of voting in the 2017 French presidential election. But when all the other parties in France close ranks to prevent the National Front from winning the second round, it's hardly a victory for democracy. And even in that bulwark of stability, Germany, the upstart Alternative for Germany beat German Chancellor Angela Merkel's Christian Democratic Union into second place in her own backyard.

JOHN KOLESIDIS / REUTERS

A clash outside the Labor Ministry in Athens, Greece, January 2013.

But there is also a left-wing version of this phenomenon. Consider the Scottish National Party (the clue is in the name), which has annihilated every other political party in Scotland, or Podemos in Spain, which has won 69 out of 350 seats in the Spanish parliament. Left-wing upstart Syriza runs Greece—even if it's under Troika tutelage—and Die Linke in Germany is yet another drain on the vote share of the once- dominant Social Democrats, whose own vote share has utterly collapsed.

These parties of course have very different policy stances. The new right favors nationals over immigrants and has, at best, a rather casual relationship with the liberal understanding of human rights. The new left, in contrast, favors redistribution from top to bottom and inclusive rather than exclusionary growth policies. But they also have more in common than we think. They are all pro-welfare (for some people, at least), anti-globalization, and most interestingly, pro-state, and although they say it sotto voce on the right, anti-finance. To see why, consider our second issue.

At the end of World War II, the United States and its allies decided that sustained mass unemployment was an existential threat to capitalism and had to be avoided at all costs. In response, governments everywhere targeted full employment as the master policy variable—trying to get to, and sustain, an unemployment rate of roughly four percent. The problem with doing so, over time, is that targeting any variable long enough undermines the value of the variable itself—a phenomenon known as Goodhart's law.

Long before Goodhart, an economist named Michal Kalecki had already worked this out. Back in 1943, he argued that once you target and sustain full employment over time, it basically becomes costless for labor to move from job to job. Wages in such a world will have to continually rise to hold onto labor, and the only way business can accommodate that is to push up prices. This mechanism, cost-push inflation, where wages and prices chase each other up, emerged in the 1970s and coincided with the end of the Bretton Woods regime and the subsequent oil shocks to produce high inflation in the rich countries of the West in the 1970s. In short, the system undermined itself, as both Goodhart and Kalecki predicted. As countries tried harder and harder to target full employment, the more inflation shot up while profits fell. The 1970s became a kind of "debtor's paradise." As inflation rose, debts fell in real terms, and labor's share of national income rose to an all-time high, while corporate profits remained low and were pummeled by inflation. Unions were powerful and inequality plummeted.

The era of neoliberalism is over. The era of neonationalism has just begun.

But if it was a great time to be a debtor, it was a lousy time to be a creditor. Inflation acts as a tax on the returns on investment and lending. Unsurprisingly in response, employers and creditors mobilized and funded a market- friendly revolution where the goal of full employment was jettisoned for a new target—price stability, aka inflation—to restore the value of debt and discipline labor through unemployment. And it worked. The new order was called neoliberalism.

Over the next thirty years the world was transformed from a debtor's paradise into a creditor's paradise where capital's share of national income rose to an all-time high as labor's share fell as wages stagnated. Productivity rose, but the returns all went to capital. Unions were crushed while labor's ability to push up wages collapsed due to the twin shocks of restrictive legislation and the globalization of production. Parliaments in turn were reduced to tweet-generating talking shops as central banks and policy technocrats wrested control of the economy away from those elected to govern.

But Goodhart's law never went away. Just as targeting full employment undermined itself, so did making inflation the policy target.

Consider that since the 2008 crisis the world's major central banks have dumped at least $12 trillion dollars into the global economy and there is barely any inflation anywhere. Almost a quarter of all European bonds now have negative yields. Unsurprisingly, interest rates are on the floor, and if it were not for the massive purchasing of assets in the Eurozone by the European Central Bank, deflation would be systemic. In sum, we may have created a world in which deflation, not inflation, is the new normal, and that has serious political consequences, which brings us back to Trump.

ALVIN BAEZ / REUTERS

Using an ATM during a power outage in San Juan, Puerto Rico, September 2016.

In a world of disinflation, credit became very cheap and the private sector levered up—massively—with post-crisis household debt now standing at $12.25 trillion in the United States. This is a common story. Wage earners now have too much debt in an environment where wages cannot rise fast enough to reduce those debts. Meanwhile, in a deflation, the opposite of what happens in an inflation occurs. The value of debt increases while the ability to pay off those debts decreases.

Seen this way, what we see is a reversal of power between creditors and debtors as the anti-inflationary regime of the past 30 years undermines itself—what we might call "Goodhart's revenge." In this world, yields compress and creditors fret about their earnings, demanding repayment of debt at all costs. Macro-economically, this makes the situation worse: the debtors can't pay—but politically, and this is crucial—it empowers debtors since they can't pay, won't pay, and still have the right to vote.

The traditional parties of the center-left and center-right, the builders of this anti-inflationary order, get clobbered in such a world, since they are correctly identified by these debtors as the political backers of those demanding repayment in an already unequal system, and all from those with the least assets. This produces anti-creditor, pro-debtor coalitions-in- waiting that are ripe for the picking by insurgents of the left and the right, which is exactly what has happened.

In short, to understand the election of Donald Trump we need to listen to the trumpets blowing everywhere in the highly indebted developed countries and the people who vote for them.

The global revolt against elites is not just driven by revulsion and loss and racism. It's also driven by the global economy itself. This is a global phenomenon that marks one thing above all. The era of neoliberalism is over. The era of neonationalism has just begun.

Mark Blyth is Eastman Professor of Political Economy at Brown University.

© Foreign Affairs

www.ingramcontent.com/pod-product-compliance
Lightning Source LLC
Chambersburg PA
CBHW081152270326
41930CB00014B/3121